# SOUVENIRS

| AUTHOR | CLASS |
|--------|-------|
| TITLE | No |

By the same author

# SOUVENIRS

ROY FULLER

LONDON MAGAZINE EDITIONS
1980

44135688 PT

Published by London Magazine Editions
30 Thurloe Place, London SW7
© Roy Fuller
SBN 904388 30 1


Printed in Great Britain
by Unwin Brothers Ltd, Old Woking, Surrey

# Contents

To my brother John
who should have written it

# 1. Jeux

As I start an explanatory note about the genesis of these memoirs of my childhood and youth, thinking that so truncated a life and brief a narrative ought to be thus prefaced, I remember that the table in the dining-room of my grandparents' house, soon to be mentioned, was on one occasion an operating table. I believe I was twelve when my mother decided I should undergo a tonsillectomy and this for some reason I cannot fathom was to take place while we were staying at the house in Hollins Road, Oldham, though we had lived for some years in Blackpool. My mother may have had knowledge from the past about the doctor concerned, or perhaps my grandfather urged his claims, possibly as a pillar of the Conservative Club. I had stayed in bed, breakfastless, on the morning in question, but when at last I was summoned for the ordeal I saw that the green table-cloth had been removed, as though I was going to use my water-colours or indian ink, and a sheet substituted.

I had a general anaesthetic and when I woke found myself on the sofa under the dining-room window from which, kneeling, I used on normal days to watch people going in and out of the little park, likely catching a glimpse of Ernest's lean, almost ragged figure. Probably I had been carried there by the doctor and the anaesthetist, if there was one. I felt terribly sick and was sick: tonsillectomy is (or was) messy, and for minor surgery comparatively risky, because of the impossibility of staunching the blood. But later in the day, and despite the soreness, I ate a boiled egg. Though set in the mid-twenties the scene seems Victorian; some Academy picture: "A Young Life Preserved".

This was actually my second tonsillectomy. The then-considered harmful appendages had been removed in infancy but had grown again. The doctor of the second operation was critical of the first: unless the *roots* of tonsils were thoroughly excised these twin foci of infection *would* re-establish themselves. He himself would ensure that this time the knife, so to speak, plunged deep enough. An additional eradication was to be performed. An eye-tooth, seemingly surplus to requirements, had grown out of the gum above existing teeth. Though I realised something would eventually have to be done about this, cowardice stopped me from initiating any action; indeed, I had developed a habit of smiling, even laughing, with my lips closed (an accomplishment that would have been useful at the theatrical treat later bestowed by the Boss), to prevent my mother being reminded to take me to the

10

dentist. However, I think it was she who mentioned the tooth to the doctor. I was greatly impressed by his confident promise to remove it on his way to the tonsils—that he should have the skills and implements for the job. Again, how antediluvian seems the absence of orthodontics in the life of the middle-class, albeit rather lower middle-class.

The book that follows grew from the chapter "Long Time a Child", which in its original form was commissioned by a magazine for a series on writers' family life. Some time after writing the piece it seemed to me I might, and ought to, continue a little further. A pattern of introspection, comedy, and the ills that flesh is heir to, had already been set, so that though there is chronological progression, the book (for the continuation itself continued) essentially partakes of the nature of a set of variations. This may be seen in the tonsillectomy episode just related, which (in a couple of senses) had its roots in infancy, involved boyhood and then went on into adolescence and beyond—for after I left school I suffered severe attacks of tonsillitis, at least one occasion bordering on quinsies, if not actually reaching that torture, and the doctor of those later days wanted to remove my tonsils for the third time, a course by then I had enough status to resist. Luckily it was not the school doctor who was involved, a big, moustached, masterful Scot who once, looking at a boil on my cheek, said: "Aye, I'll just ease that", fumbling in his waistcoat pocket and producing what proved to be a portable scalpel, the unscrewable blade being reversed and fitted into the handle when carried. The ensuing scar is visible to this day: the absence of hygiene had no ill effect, however.

I seem to think Dr. MacFarland lived and had his surgery in the very street in which the school was situated: certainly my friend Leslie and his mother's house was there, a house they shared at that time with the uncle who later drew Bartok from the air. And as to that carbuncular epoch, I have somehow had to omit mention of another boy who became a friend, though less close than Leslie, called Charles Edward Emanuel Fahmy. I have changed the surname as I have done throughout where an actual name might cause pain or embarrassment. Fahmy arrived at school when already fifteen or sixteen, typical of the exotic boarder the school would catch in greater numbers in its palmier days. Though he was an Egyptian—or at any rate lived there: the clash of forenames with surname rather mysterious—his English was first-class and he was contumelious about the ability in that sphere of the headmaster of his previous school in Alexandria, whose notion of idiomatic English was to say as rapidly as my grandfather repeating the ice-cream recipe given anon: "Very nice, very good, very nice for the bally vater-closet." Thinking of the impregnable Boss, this ignorant folly on the part of a headmaster struck me as strange indeed.

I refer subsequently to one's personal sense of the significant autobiographical detail, and the misgivings about trying to share it. In certain instances there is an historical or archeological element, slight reminders or revelations of the past which have intrinsic interest. I might have written, for example, with not much guilt about the risk of boring, of Jack Hylton, who in very early days starred in the pierrots in Happy Valley; his father, also on view, being the impresario of the troupe. Later "Jack Hylton and His Band" appeared at the "Palace Varieties", famous enough to take up the whole of the "second half". The big band sound of special timbre was to be heard for some seconds before the foot-lighted curtain rose, causing my Uncle Freddy (visiting us at the time) to remark justly on the formicating frisson these aural and visual effects induced. Later Jack Hylton himself became an impresario, but on a scale far beyond his father, though by then he had strangely come to resemble the elderly man who used to mooch about Happy Valley. I could also have expanded experiences in the theatre. My paternal grandmother was said to have been a Spanish dancer, but perhaps everyone lays claim to some romantic forebear. In any case, as will be seen, I inherited a sufficient taste for the boards from my mother's side. I wonder how many remember as vividly as I do Cora Goffin (marvellous Jamesian name, now overlain by the distinguished but more commonplace cognomen Lady Littler): an extremely pretty girl, excellent dancer on excellent legs, with a more than passable voice, usually taking the lead in Number One touring companies of twenties musical comedies like *Princess Charming*.

But this is degenerating into an old buffer's chain of consciousness. One or two links more must be added, however, though the last thing one wants to do is to impose a method of reading the book or give away such game as it possesses. Certain musical compositions have

13

been made out of wisps of themes, fitted together simply where practicable (as it appears) and scarcely repeated. One says "compositions" but perhaps a single work is in mind, *Jeux*. Not for the first time one thinks apropos of creativity: if only one had been a composer! As in life, the scenario of the ballet has its strong elements of the commonplace not to say ludicrous—"a park, a game of tennis, the chance encounter of two girls and a young man in pursuit of a lost tennis ball" (as Debussy in part described it)—yet the music's final effect is enigmatic and elusive. During the writing of my later pages I read for the first time *The Education of Henry Adams*, with increasing dismay at the grasp the author shows of his life, particularly of its broad intellectual turns and advances. Here, that side of things is more or less confined to such discoveries as that the title of the sad song "Vale", often sung in the drawing-rooms of childhood, was not pronounced like "veil", an item of women's attire still quite popular at the time—and the subject of a joke I think told by Fred Walmsley which I found memorably funny. Two women are eating tripe in a restaurant and one remarks: "This tripe's tough." Says the other: "You wouldn't find it so tough, dear, if you pushed your veil up."

· During my life various kinds of enigmas or conundrums have come into fashion, been worked to death, and then forgotten. "There's no Owen Nares," I used solemnly to say to grown-ups, he being a celebrated matinée idol of the time. When this was challenged as contrary to reality (the challenger nevertheless uneasily feeling in a dotty kind of way that one so handsome might possibly

14

be a waxwork or automaton), the explanation followed that indeed there was no "o" in Nares. Rather later, the catch took the form of a question about a popular song, such as "Do you know the big horse song?" "No, what's that?" *"Because I Love You."* Coincidentally it comes to mind that this number was in the repertoire of Layton and Johnstone, favourites of Auntie Vi.

Recalling, or trying to recall, riddles—that not too badly describes the autobiographical process, conducted as it is in my case with the most meagre of source material. Nor, of course, is the past frozen in the mind, to be dug out in lumps like ice, some fragmented in the doing. Rather, it goes on changing until the end of life. Only the other day did I read that 1911 was Coronation Year, with a summer of exceptional heat. In that season I was conceived (my young parents' first child) in circumstances—perhaps of *al fresco* curiousness—no one now can ever know.

# 2. Long Time A Child

My father and his sister were brought up in Caithness in circumstances that have never been clear to me. They were "remittance children", probably illegitimate, destined for a life far above the station of the family that looked after them. Early photographs show them prosperously, even ornately, dressed, looking out with aplomb. Then the remittances stopped, perhaps in their early teens, and they came south to Manchester or its immediate environs where there was a business connection with the family that had reared them. Both children proved extremely capable. My aunt, Minnie, became Matron (or possibly merely Assistant Matron) of the Manchester Royal Infirmary at, I should judge, a remarkably early age. My father, Leopold, twenty-seven or twenty-eight at the date of my birth in 1912, was then assistant works manager of a rubber-proofing mill just outside Manchester. Later he became a director. Both

16

children must, in their late teens and early twenties, have addressed themselves energetically to making a way in the world, rather as if they were native small-town Scots of the epoch. Minnie's career speaks for itself. I have a copy of *Vanity Fair* awarded to my father "for success in Practical Inorganic Chemistry" during the 1904-05 session by the Manchester School of Technology which presumably he attended out of working hours. I have also (in a sparse collection of relics) a notebook he kept as a young man, in his elegant and masterful hand, of stock exchange speculations mostly in options and for comically small sums, obviously all he could afford to risk. His interest in rubber plantation shares persisted, for I recall them being discussed when I was a boy: they were low-priced and highly speculative, and presumably he knew something about the demand for and price of the product—ideal subjects for a flutter.

At every age his photographs show him to have possessed quite startlingly good looks. Blonde as a child, his hair later turned dark and wavy; his complexion as an adult was of the olive kind; nose straight, lips well-formed; eyes light rather than dark. This appearance was often thought to be "foreign": it caused consternation to my maternal grandfather when my mother introduced her fiancé or intended fiancé to her family. My grandfather was always greatly suspicious of anything alien to his own way of life or at any rate the way of life of the English provincial establishment. It must have been as late as the time of the first labour administration that I heard him grudgingly admit that the gang of Labour politicians in local government owned at least a simian cleverness.

At the time of my mother's marriage in 1910 my grandfather, Fred Broadbent, must already have been Superintendent Registrar of Births, Marriages and Deaths for Oldham, the industrial town seven miles to the north-east of Manchester. He had previously been Master of Oldham Workhouse, before that Clerk to the Master, and a good while before that a schoolmaster, though I guess his academic qualifications were minimal. The story goes that a qualification for the initial work-house post was the ability to play for the services in the workhouse chapel, an accomplishment he falsely claimed. When it was put to the test he played a few elementary chords on the organ (probably with the restricted fingers to be hereafter mentioned), my grandmother diverting attention with her expert voice. My mother used some-times to surprise people momentarily by observing that she had been born in the workhouse, as was literally the case. She had a repertoire of stories of those days, some scatological: the effect of the sudden richness of the beer and plum pudding served for Christmas dinner on the internal economy of the geriatric inmates; the simpleton who used to collect the ordure from the lavatories upset-ting his wheeled bin and interspersing his bare-handed scooping-up with bites from a piece of bread—someone my Uncle John's father-in-law might have found useful in later days, as will appear.

There were a few books in my grandparents' house (notably, from my point of view, Austin Freeman's *The Singing Bone*) and my grandfather probably borrowed

18

from the public library, for he was once heard to say that he liked a good novel (which he pronounced "nuvvle"), instancing Donn Byrne (a middle-brow writer who may now be forgotten) as a purveyor of that commodity. He was a Justice of the Peace, active in local politics, a Tory Councillor, later an Alderman, and in 1924–25 Mayor of the Borough. Yet he was essentially an indolent man, though plainly not lacking application and ability in areas of life that interested him. Perhaps his talent was for "play" rather than work. He was, for instance, very keen on bridge which he played both at home and at the local Conservative club. At home at least he would punctuate the game with remarks, often quotations (as were not a few of his remarks in general conversation). When playing an obviously losing hand and his opponents got the lead, trumps exhausted, he might, for example, say: "The curse never fell upon our nation until now." He showed in other contexts familiarity with the text of *The Merchant of Venice,* very likely a hangover from his pedagogical days.

I know my brother will not mind my saying that he and I often recognize in ourselves these and other characteristics of our maternal grandfather. (In my case I feel I have become more and more like him in physique and habits as the years have gone by, though even as boys we imitated him—sometimes to the extent of tucking the two outer fingers of each hand into the palm when playing cards or raising a glass, for he suffered from the shrinking of the tissues known as Dupuytrin's Contracture.) I would include a certain recklessness about gaining personal advantage. And about personal dignity. Both my

19

grandparents had catarrh (Oldham is high, cold and damp: good for cotton-spinning, bad for human respiration). When in the mornings of 1924–25 the mayoral limousine arrived to take my grandfather to his duties he might not immediately enter the door held open by the chauffeur but go behind the car to expectorate into the gutter the phlegm raised by the sudden influx of outside air to his chest. There may well have been a conscious element of self-deflation in this: his accent always became very broad when encountering proletarian characters (and being so well known in his various avatars his progress in the street was a succession of such encounters: " 'Ow do, Fred?" " 'Ow do, Albert?") Though two of his brothers, James and Newton, did well for themselves, he never had any more money than his salary and pension, and lived in simple circumstances. As time went on I think he grew fond of my father and certainly appreciated aspects of the latter's rapidly changing life-style. "Leo spoilt my taste for cheap cigars," he once said. He lit and smoked an occasional cigarette almost as carefully and daintily as a cigar, the mode accentuated by the limited number of fingers available.

Emily Jenkins (her maiden name), my maternal grandmother, had a background even humbler than my grandfather's. Her father had been a regular soldier, had served in the Crimean War, had ended up as Sergeant. At one time, presumably as a pensioner, he had had a newspaper round, my grandmother acting as delivery girl—shoeless and stockingless, according to tradition (though that would not have been uncommon at the epoch in question: I myself as a boy saw barefoot children

20

in Oldham). Later she worked as a mill-girl, probably in a cotton-spinning factory. She had an outstanding singing voice, was in a church choir at the age of eight and as a young teenager was invited to join a small paid church choir as leader. She had acting ability, too, and before she was married rejected, on the advice of the old stick-in-the-mud parson at her church, the chance of a stage career. After bringing up five children and playing her part in public and charitable affairs, in old age she took up drawing and painting, mostly of the "automatic" kind. Her talent in this line was not great but the facility had blossomed in two of her sons, who were adroit amateur technicians in the graphic arts. Most of her children could sing and act. My mother inherited "a good voice", as they used to say—a mezzo-soprano, as I imagine my grandmother's to have initially been—but in the years after her marriage employed it only for occasional domestic purposes.

My grandparents owned an HMV gramophone whose beautifully made oak horn probably indicated that it was a good machine of its epoch, which may, however, have been somewhat remote. Though I remember my youngest uncle bringing home Luigini's *Ballet Égyptien* as a hair-raising sample of the new technique of "electrical" recording, I do not recall records at an earlier date other than of band music and such things as a Harry Lauder song and monologue called "When I Was Twenty-one", occupying a single-sided black-label HMV record, most of which I still have off by heart, or had a few years ago. (Lauder, in the role of a boozy Scot, accounted for his high colour by what even in those remote days I thought

21

of as a remarkably poetic trope: "I ate too much red cabbage and the vinegar never left ma face.") However, I suppose the restricted repertoire I remember may have been the result of my own reiterated selection from the available discs. I was at least fourteen (probably fifteen) before I listened properly to classical music, but I did quite soon become attuned to what may be termed "pier-end" music, having regard to the limited modes of dissemination of the times.

The first house my parents took and in which I was born I had imagined to be of the terrace kind, opening straight on to the street. When my son was teaching at Manchester University I went to find this and other houses in the district I had known as a child. I had more than half expected my birthplace in Timpson Street, Failsworth (an urban district between Manchester and Oldham), to have disappeared in some slum clearance scheme. Not a bit of it: the house proved to be well-built, of red brick, semi-detached, with a little front garden—small but perfectly respectable. How odd to stand there, a middle-aged man, with the far memories of my infantile life in the house, notably of being under the dining-table with a neighbour's female child, hidden by the table-cloth (in style similar to my grandparents' but with a blue pile), the feeling-tone being of excited love. But the house stayed strange, brought no additional recall.

My father was quick to make his material surroundings reflect his progress in his career. By the time my surviving brother was born in 1916 we had moved into Oldham itself, to a bigger house in a "better" neighbourhood—a long road called Frederick Street. Opposite was an open space where the terrain fell, giving a good view of the smoking factory and huddled domestic chimneys of the area, a few miles away, from which we had elevated ourselves.

Quite impossible to recover what immediately emotional or more enduring effects the 1914–18 War had on a small child. Naturally I was well aware of the war's existence, wondering, as my father read the paper at breakfast, how it would find enough news to fill its pages when the war was over. One of my uncles, a mere lad, was in the Army, but I do not recall the family anxiety. Nor do I remember anything of the second son, born to my parents in 1914, who died when a few weeks old through an undiagnosed genetic effect in the pylorus, preventing the natural emptying of the stomach into the intestine—a defect curable by a quite simple operation. Surely there were affects in the little outliver. The birth of my surviving brother, my parents' third son, I do have a memory of—my mother still in bed in a front bedroom of the Frederick Street house, the new infant in a cot with a muslin canopy, my mother reading to me from a paperback volume of fairy tales, a regularly-published series often bought for me. I would have been almost four years and four months old. I suspect that the occasion was the result of my demand for attention or, more likely, my mother's way of indicating my continuing importance—and remembered because of this. Indeed, I am convinced I could read for myself before my surviving brother was born: surely I was alone with my father and mother (in the front seat of the family motor-car) when

23

I read my first word—OXO—from an advertisement hoarding, a feat which surprised me almost as much as my parents.

The rubber-proofing mill did well during the war, with government contracts for ground-sheets and the like. My father became a shareholder in and a director of the private company that owned it. It was probably in 1919 (though it could have been 1918) that we moved to a house in Waterhead, on the extreme outskirts of Oldham, in fact just over the Lancashire border with Yorkshire. Beyond lay the moorland of the Pennines: my bedroom looked out on its vivid green and the black dry-stone walls that ran over it and I recall lugging a crimson-bound volume of *Chums* up to that window to catch the last light as I read illegally after going to bed. The road the house was in led through the moorland to tiny grey-black manufacturing towns in the steep valleys, a landscape that still seems to me mysterious and haunting—just as the mill-dominated streets of urban east Lancashire, so long quitted, remain, as the phrase goes, my spiritual home.

The Waterhead house struck me at the time as being very grand. It stood high above the road and had a name and no number. I was proud of being seen proprietorially opening the front gate on which the name was painted. It was in fact, as I saw on the pilgrimage already mentioned, a mock-Tudor house typical of many built in Edwardian times or slightly later for the professional class. It was commodious enough for my brother and me to have a day nursery, with a cupboard each for books and toys, which gave me strangely keen pleasure. Into

24

my cupboard went *Tales from Sir Walter Scott,* a present from my Aunt Minnie, hangover from her Caithness upbringing. My father had had the floor laid with a patent green material which I remember him proclaiming was as hard-wearing as linoleum yet warm and quite resilient to the touch: ideal for bare knees, as a foundation for Lotts' bricks and Hornby train lines. There were two maids but I do not think both of them lived in. The chauffeur certainly did not live in.

I wonder if the chauffeur were not acquired only after my father's illness, when the strain must have been great of driving the now not inconsiderable distance from home to work and back. My father made a will on April 9, 1920, and that may have immediately preceded the colostomy he underwent to alleviate the bowel cancer he had been found to have. I remember the day he went for the operation and I do not think he was driven by Smith. After great suffering my father died on December 18, 1920. He was thirty-six, my mother thirty-two. I think my mother was pregnant with her fourth son before my father's illness was diagnosed: at any rate, the child was born not long before my father's death. Like my first brother, it suffered from the pyloric defect and died after a few weeks' unhappy life. I remember it being said later, probably by my mother, that they tried to take as little account as possible of the baby's death because of my father's desperate condition.

Of course, my father's appearance changed devastatingly during his illness. I have been told he was extremely courageous in his final months, for a time continuing to play bridge—a great passion—though afterwards he

25

might have to go on hands and knees upstairs to bed. It was a source of sadness to him that towards the end I was afraid of him. I wonder whether that was the emotion or whether it was not, already at that age, compassion so extreme as to amount to cowardice. I was certainly afraid of him after his death, seeing the closed door of what had doubtless become a dreaded bedroom, wondering if the body were still there. There was no full disclosure to the boy of eight and three-quarters of the appearance and facts of death, as presumably there would have been in Victorian times. I was sent to stay with friends for some days, covering the period of the funeral. One evening, while there, I messed my pants, an indication, as I see now, of the troubled state beneath the pleasure at sharing the play of the two little girls of the family, but then a wholly enigmatic event, causing me immense embarrassment. It seems clear that I was already an introverted character, whose tender heart went frustratingly with a distaste for displays of emotion, indeed for anything much disturbing the commonplace routines of life. Apart from being a "bad" boy I suppose I could not have had a nature less helpful to my mother in the ruins of her life.

My father had been fond of the Fylde coast— accustomed to the sea in his Scottish boyhood—and for several years had taken a furnished house in Blackpool (then, certainly at its "North Shore", still possessing a degree of "tone") for a month or so in the summer, he himself commuting when his own holiday period had expired. It was to live in "rooms" in one of those houses that we (my mother, my surviving brother and myself) went initially following my father's death, after the house and furniture were sold, the maids and chauffeur dismissed. The landlady, Mrs. Vero, and her son were of course in residence with us (we had not the whole house as for one of the previous summer holidays) and they were the first I recall of the Dickensian characters encountered in my mother's wanderings during the rest of my life with her. The son, perhaps in his early twenties, played Rachmaninov's notorious piano prelude so assiduously that I still refer to the piece as "Willie Vero". He frequently did dialogues in assumed bass and falsetto voices (a talent also possessed by Dickens's Sloppy), usually with persecutory Pinterish undertones. One dialogue began on the following lines:

> Bass voice: "Where are the papers?"
> Falsetto voice: "What papers?"
> Bass voice: "Those secret papers."    Etc.

The characters seem Dickensian not only because of the essential truth in Dickens's vision but also because of our forced and usually fleeting relationship with them, sometimes as fleetingly renewed. At a later epoch we lived in a Blackpool private hotel where the passing show was concentratedly thronged, swift and varied. My sense of the ludicrous in human character and action is possessed by my brother even more sharply, perhaps because his power of observation is keener.

We left the Vero household to return to Oldham to a house my mother bought not far from my grandparents. I guess she was encouraged in this move by them. The

27

house was not even up to Frederick Street standards, as I think my mother was morbidly aware.

My father's shares in the rubber-proofing mill, and other possessions, eventually realised sufficient for my mother to live on without working and to educate my brother and me. Our way of life was modest and my mother, without being at all specific in the matter, always made me conscious of the limits of her resources, so that my possibly native parsimony was reinforced by a real fear of the money running out. At the end of my school-days, for example, when I was sixteen, what was presented was the opportunity to qualify as a professional man, so I was articled to a solicitor. The speculative job in journalism or training in art (either of which would then have met my own deepest wishes) would not have fulfilled the plan my mother had conceived to manage her money so as to launch both her sons safely into adult life. As it happened, this cautious view—sustained by consultations with equally unimaginative or ignorant friends—could scarcely have been more ill-suited to the talents possessed by her children. Though my brother and I both made successful careers (mine slightly more conventional than his), only when we have moved into spheres somewhat away from them have we begun to show our true abilities. In my case at least, such movement has almost always been at the behest of others. My father's death shattered my mother's existence: it also caused his children to lead lives that were for many years divided and too narrow in scope.

One psychologizes about oneself in this way with apparent confidence but may be wide of the mark.

Possibly no amount of lift-off which public school, university and money—and a standard English accent and *savoir faire*—would have provided could have changed the dominating part of my personality: shy, intellectual, naive to the point of gormlessness (archetypally poetic, one might say) and not badly summed up in the well-known phrase by Hartley Coleridge I happened to light on while writing this: "Long time a child and still a child."

I must also make it clear that the petty bourgeois life—carless, servantless, seats in the pit rather than the dress circle—to which we were suddenly returned was far from uncongenial to me. Many of my most enjoyable hours were spent at my grandparents' house where in the front room, nominally the dining-room but used as a living room, there was a square table with a scrubbed top, normally covered by a green plush cloth with a fringe. This latter would be replaced by a white cloth for meals; and after a lunch of, say, hot-pot (baked best-end of neck chops, sliced potatoes and onions) and apple pie (with Lancashire cheese—prize, of course) the white cloth would be removed and a newspaper laid down so that I could draw or paint. At a later epoch I might be joined in this by my grandmother: she with her free style, me probably copying something I had squared up from *Chatterbox* or a coloured post-card. My mother's siblings and their spouses and children also gave pleasure, providing social life without too many accompanying pangs of shyness.

A good few catch-phrases and memories, perhaps setting the whole tone of one's attitude to everyday

29

existence, predominantly comic as it must be, have survived from that period. I think of the only child of my mother's elder sister, slightly younger than me, who was a proverbial source. At the (silent) cinema she would say out loud, as much because of her infantile incomprehension of plot as innocence about sexual mores: "What's that man doing to that lady?"—an annoying phrase then but useful today when confronted by the narrative obfuscations of modern film and television drama.

I should emphasize that these memories of my grandparents' house are not confined to the time of my mother's return to Oldham. That come-back was so unsuccessful that with phenomenal rapidity she sold the house and we went back to rooms in Blackpool. It could be that she was less pleased than I was to be close to her parents. (it was some time before the penny dropped and I saw her as an attractive widow who despite her fidelity to her children and to my father's memory was capable of fresh personal attachments). There were other relatives at hand near her own age but the friends of Waterhead days had largely fallen off, not to be wondered at in the utterly changed circumstances. She had acquired friendships in Blackpool during the annual visits there and I daresay they seemed more congenial and, potentially at least, more accessible. Was my own particular area of unhappiness taken into account by her? During our short return stay in Oldham I attended the local board school whose great bleak playgrounds, vast numbers and strange routines (as they all seemed to me) were purgatory after my previous experience of genteel dames' schools. Back in Blackpool I returned happily to a girls' school where boys were taken in the lower forms—until I was too old for it and went to a private boarding school. Strangely enough I should almost certainly have been better off in the local authority system: I was a good examinee but my private school never entered boys for university scholarships. Moreover, though it is nice to be coddled I have got along quite well at various epochs as an unprivileged member of society.

Our accommodation in Blackpool was not in the Vero household, though nearby. (Perhaps the Vero rooms were not available or my mother had wearied of the Prelude in C sharp minor.) We occupied the new place for what seems in retrospect—and seemed then—a long time, though was probably no more than a couple of years. Our landlady, Miss Barraclough, was a gigantically fat woman who slept in her kitchen and never bathed. I still often repeat (and not now wholly in jest) a phrase of idiomatic construction employed by her to indicate her sense of the woes of the world pressing down on her: "Dearie me today." In the side part of the garden, adjoining the street, was a small billboard that showed the weekly attractions of a local cinema, called "The Imperial". This display entitled her to two seats gratis at Monday matinées, to which, during school holidays, I often accompanied her; Miss Barraclough's "free pass" seeming to me an astonishing bounty. Strange pair. I think she invariably wore a navy-blue "costume" of thin, shiny serge, through which the projecting upper rim of her corset was almost as visible as when she was without a jacket indoors. Thus, and at others of Blackpool's

31

numerous cinemas, was sustained—developed, rather—my passion for that art.

It was only to be expected that my mother's health should have declined during all these events. She was by no means a chronic complainer but I was aware of her "nerves" (the term in *The Waste Land* was in common use, perhaps still is) and later of her "palpitations". Concern about her physical well-being grew to be as nagging as the concern that we were not drawing on capital. Rentier's worries, communicating themselves in classic manner even to the younger members of the family—they would get no sympathy today, but were real and painful. Later my mother's symptoms assumed rather more obvious physical forms and very belatedly she was diagnosed as having Graves' Disease—hyperthyroidism—and underwent, just before the Second World War, a partial thyroidectomy, then a perilous operation.

She died in 1949. A good many years after her death I became more and more troubled by irregular beating of the heart. The electrocardiograph and other tests showed no organic cardiac trouble. A consultant soon diagnosed Graves' Disease. "Are you nervous?" was one question asked. Almost without hesitation, rapidly reviewing my ancestry, character and behaviour, I said: "Yes"—though at the time I was at the broadest stretch of my scope and responsibility as a lawyer. In fact my "nerves" were doubtless efficiently concealed behind the mask by then perfected for presentation to the ordinary encounters of life.

Defects are inescapably inherited: it is more difficult

to see or appreciate the compensations that accompany them. Some sort of soft centre, such as my mother possessed (and I should add that she was totally unintellectual), is surely almost essential to a poet: he must also have intelligent ability, the quality my father seemed to own in abundance. I dare say he was also not without imaginative insight. One of my few memories of him is of his taking me to the dentist for an extraction or extractions—in those days, in that place, a far from painless procedure. Afterwards we went to a stationer's shop, where he bought me a large black-japanned tin of water-colour paints. On another occasion when we were out together he announced that we would go to see the pictures. My spirits rose, anticipating the entertainment later offered by the Imperial. To my initial disappointment we went into the Oldham Municipal Art Gallery. Could it have been on that early visit that the enormous and then famous canvas of Cleopatra applying the asp to her bosom made its mark on me? Perhaps its sensuous splendours were something my father particularly wanted to see, following the line indicated by his acquisition of the illustrated Macaulay I will refer to again.

I am slightly surprised to recall that my father also took me to Watersheddings and Boundary Park, the respective homes of the Oldham rugby league and association football clubs—surprised only because of the brief time I seem in retrospect to have spent with him, for I have inherited his broad interest in watching sport. I see us approaching the Watersheddings ground over some well-trodden cindered "tips", yet any tone and details of the relations between us have dropped completely away.

33

I hope I concentrated on and responded to the proceedings to the best of my puerile ability, giving him a bit of confidence about my future nous. Would we ever have seriously clashed had he survived into my adolescence and beyond? Or would he simply have had to put up with my withdrawn evasiveness, like many another? His own character is to me essentially elusive. Presumably his talent for management and decision-taking was not, like mine, vitiated by a species of pusillanimity—too great a facility for seeing another's point of view, an almost morbid concern for another's feelings; qualities which assort oddly with ruthlessness in sticking to unpopular positions and resolves.

I might put a word in here about my father's great attachment to his home, a trait almost on the exaggerated lines of that of Mr. Woodhouse, and appearing again in my brother and myself. In my father's case the cause may have been his parentless upbringing: in his sons the cause perhaps his own early death. The patterns over the generations may be somewhat mystical, however. A few years after my father died I had a septic right index finger as a result of which the nail came off. The new nail, when grown, appeared down one side as though detached from the circumambient flesh. My mother said that this nail was exactly like that on my father's right index finger.

Apart from the chemistry prize already mentioned, my father's books (of no vast number) were disposed of immediately after his death (my mother was the reverse of a hoarder). Among them I recall John Buchan's *Greenmantle*—a title that seemed strange and reverberant to me as a boy of seven or eight—and Macaulay's *Lays of Ancient Rome*. These two works may well have indicated the parameters of his literary taste. Indeed, the Macaulay seems not altogether in character—more like the taste or early enforced reading of my grandfather, whose sayings included a number of quotations from the poet Thomas Campbell, one I put in the Macaulay class. The *Lays*, as mentioned, had line illustrations of an occasional anatomical explicitness, a bit like the work of Flaxman, and that perhaps accounted for its presence in my father's bureau.

I had a fair number of books of my own in the Waterhead days and do not remember poaching on any of my father's. It might have surprised him (and surely would have pleased him) to have discovered, had he lived, the eventual maturing of my taste in that area. To translate my lust for reading into the practical terms of buying books would have been just up his alley (and as I write this I am reminded that my brother has been a book-accumulator all his life, and in his own field a notable collector). How pure (if tedious for others) is pride in one's children! I deeply regret that my mother died before such honours and positions as I possess came, almost inevitably, to me: she would have seen them as justification of her care and application—and educational policy—during those early years.

I ought not to omit adding that the puzzlement to me of the Caithness childhood was not helped by my Aunt Minnie, I feel sure even before my father died, marrying an Australian (I believe a patient in her hospital) and moving to what was thought of as the outback and

35

possibly was. She never returned. After bearing two or three children she died prematurely of cancer like my father. But even had I met her again in my later life would I have catechised her about the past? I doubt it. I see now that even my mother might have illuminated many questions had she been asked. The character I possessed that soft-pedalled interrogation will sufficiently emerge.

# 3.  Comics

*There move the enormous comics, drawn from life.*
W.H. Auden

---

It must have been in 1923, when I was eleven, that I went to boarding-school in Blackpool. What could have been in my mother's mind? (It would have been easy for me to be a day-boy because the house where we had "rooms" was no more than three or four miles from the school). It could scarcely have been to free her for some amatory relationship, for my brother remained at home (though it is true he was four years younger than I). I feel that it was simply for my social and educational amelioration—perhaps my father had in his lifetime spoken of "boarding-school" as desirable for his children, though the school chosen by my mother was far from what he might have had in mind, conscious as he always seemed to have been of the importance of solid quality

37

in what he got for his growing income. If some friend had recommended the place to her the advice was not far-sighted. There were two sizeable boys' "private" schools in the town: the one I went to was shortly to be on the downgrade; the other eventually became a public-school, of however minor an example.

The nature of the school I joined (and stayed with until the end of my schooldays) will likely be unfamiliar fifty years on. On arrival I was put in Form 2b, so that there must have been boys of only nine or ten in Form 1. At the other end of the school were boys of sixteen, possibly seventeen. At first there were about seventy day-boys and thirty boarders. The numbers declined but the school always ranged beyond prep school scope. One could stay to take matriculation (as the leaving exami-nation then was), though no boy in my time proceeded to university. Undoubtedly the school traded on the gentility principle: in those days it conferred a higher social status (if only temporarily) than the state schools, and in the case of day boys for a modest cost. It probably also took boys who had failed to pass into grammar schools. No exaggerated social snobbery was involved, however. Thinking at random, one of my contemporaries became a woman's hairdresser, another a coalman (though both were self-employed).

Why the boarders came is a more complex question. A few were foreign or the sons of parents abroad. One or two were so gormless that their parents were no doubt glad to have them taken off their hands and somehow made literate that the agency was unimportant. But as to the majority of boarders I expect the school was trading on past glories, my mother's hearing of it evidence of that. One of the first things that struck me were some photographs on the dining-room walls (photographs already slightly yellowed and old-fashioned) of a school production of *Les Fourberies de Scapin*. That boys porting rapiers, in plumed hats and tights (however wrinkled) should give a play in French, to me denoted a past of great enterprise and intellect.

However, it must be said that during my time I judge the standard of teaching to have remained remarkably high. The standard was set by the Headmaster himself who never allowed any boy, however dull, to evade participation in his classes. This he achieved by *ad hominem* interrogation and, not infrequently, some kind of dramatic action. "If I were a Zulu I'd do a war dance," he said once at a boy's crass answer, later going behind the blackboard (for some obscure but strangely effective reason) to fulful the terpsichorean side of the proposition. Another time he took a boy out of the classroom and ran him round the playground "to wake him up". During his absence the class were in awestruck silence, straining to catch any sound of the two ill-assorted pairs of feet. Effective teaching was actually helped as a result of the school's decline, classes getting smaller and smaller as one progressed through the school, the sixth consisting, when I was in it, of no more than a dozen boys, if that.

My mother and I went to the school for a preliminary interview (doing the journey by tram along the promenade), though I guess my admission was not in doubt. The building was undistinguished, consisting of a pair of large semi-detached houses in a street at right-angles

39

to the promenade. The pair had been altered so as to communicate in what always remained for me a somewhat mysterious manner. On the ground floor, from the noise and I daresay squalor of the boarders' dining-room, common room and coat lobby one could reach the quiet gloom and relative opulence of the Headmaster's family quarters. The first room one came to was the Headmaster's study. Across the hall was the drawing-room, entered only on two or three curious occasions, one being the interview referred to. The rest was virtually unknown territory, as was the first floor. Did this also intercommunicate? I do not remember, perhaps never knew. One or two masters slept and had their ablutions on "the boys' side" of this floor: at the time it would have struck me as strange indeed if they could have penetrated the intimate quarters of the Headmaster and his family—though now the notion seems less outré. On the second floor, to get from one house to the other you simply walked through one of the dormitories.

The classrooms were at the rear of these two houses, in a single-storey building erected where the property was bounded by a back street. This building was extended during my early days at the school to make a science laboratory, perhaps the school's last gesture of prosperity and expansion. All the back land (not of any great extent) was eventually asphalted over as a playground, except for a small walled garden appurtenant to the Headmaster's side of the pair of houses and the "bogs", redolent during all my time at the school of one particular brand of disinfectant.

The interview took place in the Headmaster's study,

my mother and I facing him across a substantial desk. He was a handsome man, though after I had left school (perhaps on the strange occasion described later) I discovered he was not, as I had always thought, tall. His acquiline features were surmounted by thick grey hair, neatly parted and brushed, the large head carried slightly on one side, as though perpetually considering some matter of grave consequence, his own virtue and right judgement being unquestionable. I and my brother (who eventually joined me at the school) have laughed a great deal recalling the character and habits of the Headmaster, but at the time I was afraid of him. He was one of those individuals whose absence from the scene greatly lightens the spirits of more flippant beings. His nickname was (anticipating the gangster films of the coming "talkies") "the Boss", the hissed syllable indicating with sickening menace his impending arrival, even though one's occupation might be innocent. He had a deep knowledge of the weakness of boys and at this first meeting plumbed my ignorance and foolishness with one simple question. He asked me to spell "cupboard", which I failed to do.

Later in the interview my mother remarked that I was "a terrible reader". Having assessed my spelling, the Headmaster naturally did not take this colloquially and said that I should have extra lessons or special attention in this field. Though my mother explained that she merely meant that I always had my nose in a book, the Headmaster's scepticism about my literacy was not removed and, as stated, condemned me to 2b where the school's younger dunces spent a good deal of time. However, after one term in 2b I went straight to Form 3.

41

I really did read a lot, mostly rubbish, perhaps almost entirely "comics" (innocent term in those days), novellas published in such series as the Nelson Lee and Sexton Blake "Libraries", and the children's "annuals". My mother borrowed books from a local twopenny library—popular novels of the romantic kind in the main. That I did not choose any books for myself from this source shows how unenterprising I was, for it surely contained such authors as E. Phillips Oppenheim who had me under a spell a little later on. The public library was a facility that, with typical conservativism (fear of dirt and germs possibly also playing a part), it never occurred to my mother to take advantage of for either of us. In later schooldays I joined under my own steam and was stunned at the riches open access revealed.

Going to boarding-school enlarged my range of reading matter through both what was called the "boarders' library" (merely a restrictive term, for there was no similar facility for day boys) and books brought to the school by boys. For some books in early days I formed a passion: for instance, Richmal Crompton's "William" stories, then starting to come out. My enthusiasm was usually for works that especially ingratiated themselves with the reader, through cosy ideology or intense read-ableness or both. After a time a master must have seen that I was a "terrible reader" and offered books from his own collection, the first being by Ian Hay and O. Henry. He asked which I'd liked better. I said the Ian Hay (it was *Pip and Pipette*), speaking the truth though conscious that O. Henry was the more considerable literary artist. Surely all this was indicative of a lack of application and seriousness—lack of genius, it might be said—that has dogged me all my life and prevented great achievements.

A new boarder with me was a boy called Hamlet. As I write I cannot recall his Christian name but in any case I always think of him in the cigar or Shakespearean mode. Through our newness we became friendly though he was a year (or perhaps more) younger than I. He was a serious boy with a scientific bent: in adolescence he treated his pimples by injecting them with a pin with Euthymol toothpaste, a strong concoction. Despite the pimples he was not unattractive, humour lurking under the solemn style. When my brother (over four years younger than I) came to the school he got to know Hamlet quite well. It was probably my brother who observed the Euthymol experiments. They would have greatly appealed to him. In any case, my brother had a wide range of Hamletiana, for many years after school Hamlet got in touch with him. In the interim Hamlet had lived abroad as a missionary in a leper colony. Perhaps he entirely lacked friends after coming back to England (he had been the sole child of a widower or grass widower). At any rate, on Hamlet's initiative the two husbands and wives met on a number of occasions. Hamlet had married only on his return and his domestic happiness was short-lived for he very soon died of a heart attack.

This is perhaps the place to note my brother's exceptional gift for encountering figures from the past, meetings always of great hilarity in the telling given his justifiably comic view of humanity. Mr. Pemberton, the headmaster in *The Ruined Boys*, has some traits of the real head-

43

master of my boarding school. Since that novel was written at least thirty years after my schooldays I never doubted that the Headmaster was safely dead, questions of defamation and wounding not arising. At typescript stage my lawyer's instinct prompted me to check. My correspondent was the former engrossing clerk of the firm of solicitors I was articled to, whom I had kept in touch with over the years. Norman Lees told me that not only was the Headmaster still alive but still teaching. Some of the typescript's choicest bits had to go. One I recall was about the Headmaster's only too identifiable ways of addressing boys—normally by surname but on a ceremonial occasion, not without a trace of ironic regard on his part, by Christian name preceded by "Master". ("Are you off to dancing-class, Master Roy?" upon observing me in "Marlborough" jacket on a weekday). A far more alarming style was "Master" alone. ("Where are you off to, Master?") In the presence of their parents he addressed boys simply by their Christian names, quite as though this was his unvarying habit: one's name on his lips sounded at once weak and bizarre.

A little later, in a railway compartment, my brother (who said he had wept with laughter at even those reminders of past life with the Boss retained in the novel) was eyed for some time by a middle-aged man who said at last: "Isn't your name Fuller?" The man turned out to be Thompson, a contemporary of my brother's at the school and who I myself recalled as a diminutive day boy. He still lived in the town where the school was situated, and my brother naturally enquired about the

Headmaster. "He is a noble old man," said Thompson, with impressive sincerity.

After a few terms Hamlet and I drifted apart—he was below me in the school and in a different dormitory. Strange epoch of life, the immediate pre-adolescent years. Had a record been kept, no doubt some sort of progress or attitude could be discerned. As it is, the period seems merely to have continued the pleasures and worries of earlier childhood, intellectual growth confined to the utterly puerile, even reading tinged with the lower activity of collecting. "The Feats of Dormitory Three" I remember entitling a holograph magazine (perhaps of no more than one number), my cover drawing being the end view of iron bedsteads with bare feet protruding. Most of the contents—probably all—were written and illustrated by me, and what is certain is that nothing in it would have shown the slightest talent. My taste for puns was carried into my conversation, much of which was designed to amuse—as ever, though I wonder whether it was as obstipated as it certainly became in adolescence and after. One boy at least in Dormitory Three was an alert audience, a mischievous fellow (in fact, his appearance not unsimian) I will call Byng, though I rather think he was killed in the War and cannot be hurt or defamed. His butt was Ames, whose aspect strangely enough also inclined to the simian, though whereas Byng resembled one of those narrow-faced monkeys with large hairless upper lips and lower jaw, Ames had been modelled on the great anthropoids—bullet head, back humped with muscle, small puzzled eyes, dangling arms, shortish bowed legs. At one time his nickname was "Gorill", the

45

word accented as a trochee. He never used his strength to discourage Byng and his other tormentors (including me, I am sorry to say). His protest merely took the form of a verbal appeal, which in time became stylised and unvarying—"Chuck it, you rotten beggar, Byng. I wish you wo-ould. You rotten beggar." Down the years this whining litany has been shortened in my family to the first phrase of it, to be used in addressing anyone exercising oppression.

Ames was a boy of limited intellectual attainments. Today in the State system such a one might well leave school unable to read or write. As it was, the small classes plus the all-seeing eye and academic energy of the Headmaster enabled Ames to keep up, in some way and to some passable degree, with the current of school work. The exercise book containing his essays was sometimes procured by Byng for the purpose of reading aloud the literary efforts there painfully put down. It must be admitted that like Caliban Ames had a power of memorable expression exceeding what might have been expected. In a story (set as essay prep) some action of the protagonist was described in succinct but mysteriously Joycean manner: "He stooped. He stoped. He stopped." Another essay (if half or threequarters of a page can be so dignified) ended with the *jeu d'esprit*: "All done by kindness. A. P. Ames." These words, too, are still useful today, marking completion of some satisfying and satisfactory job.

Byng left prematurely and Ames's life became much more ordinary. In the end he and I were the two full backs (as they were then called) in the school's soccer

46

XI, his dogged strength making up for my deficiencies, since my speed made me an "attacking" defender, not always reliable. But this must have been in the last year of my school life when the school's shrinkage was beginning to be apparent (I was even in the cricket XI, though having a meagre talent for the game), not least in the staff. Mr. Tregenza had become senior master, a promotion that could scarcely have been foreseen. He was short, stout, as uncommunicative as I later became, possibly in his mid forties. When accompanying the boarders on their Sunday walk he sometimes held his walking-stick upright behind his back, the crook hooked on to the brim of his trilby to stop it being blow off in the stiff wind usually prevalent at Blackpool. I think originally he had taught only French but in my latter time took History as well and perhaps English also. I was never on easy terms with him but then in those days, at such a school, the wall of reserve between masters and boys was rarely breached. Strange that a master would so seldom try to gain affection as well as respect; try for perspectives other than those, such as they were, running from the curriculum. Still, the boys (coming, as almost all of them did, from thoroughly petty-bourgeois seaside town backgrounds) must have lacked the social *savoir faire* to enable them to respond to other than utterly conventional approaches, in my own case the thing aggravated by shyness and respect for rules.

Mr. Tregenza was an able pianist. Two "pieces" of his that I recall were Chopin's *Fantaisie Impromptu* and the "Andaluza" of Granados, which indicate his technical proficiency. In the evenings he often used to come across

47

to the classrooms building to play on the piano used for the morning hymn. I suppose these recitals made their mark about the time I was conscious of losing arguments with two day-boy pianists in which I foolishly maintained that compared with "pier-end" music (such things as the *Ballet Égyptien*, familiar through the Stokowski records bought by Uncle Freddy in the first days of electrical recording) classical music lacked the essential ingredient of tunes. It seemed greatly daring when at last I ventured into the actual classroom where Mr. Tregenza was playing, to sit and listen (the music was audible elsewhere, for most of the classrooms were formed by ingeniously mobile wood and glass partitions on rails, duty of the monitors to slide into place before and after morning assembly). I expect some further time elapsed before I had a few, probably laconic, conversations with him about music. I remember only two of his remarks: one that he was fed up with the *Fantaisie Impromptu* (which I had daringly requested), the other (in response to my question) that Busoni was the best pianist he had ever heard. These replies, when I ponder them, perhaps indicate a somewhat greater depth of relationship than I recall. I mean I did not initially know the name of the Chopin piece, so must have hummed its haunting central theme or otherwise with some particularity identified it. The name of Busoni stuck with me (helped by Busoni's Beethovenian head being on the cover of a piece of Mr. Tregenza's music, probably a Busonian arrangement) and many years later, coming to him again through *Music Ho!* and Bernard Van Dieren's *Down Among the Dead Men*, I wrote a longish poem about him, justly

48

unpublished; also, he lies behind the title of my first novel for adults, *The Second Curtain*. A theme of Constant Lambert's book is the desirability of a continuous tradition in music of the modern epoch—the fingerprinting and almost unconscious changing of the old forms being sufficient "progress" in the art, a notion (though I put it crudely) that has always greatly attracted me in the arts generally. Curious that the origins of this lie so far in one's past. It strikes me, too, as I write this, that I have acquired four or five discs of Granados's piano music, currently being recorded complete by the excellent pianist Thomas Rajna and still, to me, appealing. I have written a poem about that composer, also, though the non-musical interest of his being torpedoed during the 1914–18 War and perishing through needlessly trying to rescue his already-rescued wife played some part in that. I might even today remark to my wife "Mr. Tregenza used to play that" when a Chopin Scherzo, say, comes over the wireless but I must not exaggerate his repertoire and influence, for one of the two day-boy pianists referred to became a special friend, and listening to *him* play and to his gramophone records (for a boy most discriminatingly chosen) went on after we had left school.

In literature I progressed from Ian Hay and O. Henry pretty well without guidance. It was a time when good writers were famous. Perhaps G. B. Shaw, mainly because of his ideological iconoclasm, was the first contemporary to get my devotion (I see the date 1927 on the flyleaf of my copy of *Androcles*, bought some time after the enthusiasm began), but before I left school at sixteen

49

I had read Aldous Huxley and ploughed through *The Dynasts* (to indicate a range of some kind). Though I also read, for instance, the nineteenth-century Russians, it now seems incredible that writers of the past did not attract me more. I quite enjoyed the set books for various examinations but do not recall exploring much further—*Silas Marner* did not lead on to *Middlemarch*—though it must be said that the classics of English literature were sparse in the boarders' library and, indeed, elsewhere in the school. So I got to know a few books pretty thoroughly, rather like my grandfather with *The Merchant of Venice* (and in this connection, having recently refreshed my memory through my elder surviving uncle's letters, I may say that he apparently varied his Lancastrian greeting of " 'ow do?" with the somewhat more baffling "How now Tubal! what news from Genoa?").

I enjoyed without reservation the organized visits made by the school to the Shakespearean touring companies that regularly took in Blackpool. An element of a "night out", rare enough in the monastic life led by the boarders, plainly enhanced the enjoyment, but I was absorbed in the plays in the manner of their original audiences, with little or no compulsion to read the texts. It was still the epoch of Sir Frank Benson, spry enough as Caliban to climb a palm tree on the magic island and come down it head first. But he was indubitably ancient and though I saw him play Mark Antony in *Julius Caesar* and, even more incongruously, Hamlet, he later resigned himself in the latter play to the part of the Ghost. Edentulousness had made even more esoteric his mannered diction, of which I can still do a fair imitation. In his company was Robert Donat, extremely funny as Aguecheek and memorable in previous visits in smaller roles because of his fine but already asthmatic voice, wide-legged stance, and slightly Lancashire diction. Plays like *The Rivals* and *She Stoops To Conquer* were also sometimes done: they seemed of almost guilty lightness to form part, as it were, of the Boss' curriculum. However, all this intellectual taste and development now seems to me, again, characteristically unthorough, second-rate, non-critical.

In my earlier days Shakespeare did not much enter the programming of the "concerts" given by the school, of which there were two a year—one in a nearby church hall, the other unofficial (though pretty well rehearsed under one of the masters) and given on the last day of the autumn term in the classrooms building (the partitions drawn back) by the boarders, the audience being merely the staff, boarders not taking part, and those day boys who chose to come. However, in my middle years in the school the boarders did put on the play scene in the last act of *A Midsummer Night's Dream.* By some unlikely stroke (probably forced through shortage of numbers) Gorill played Hippolyta. The Wall would surely have been more appropriate—though come to think of it Hippolyta had, to be sure, once been Queen of the Amazons, a physically robust past the master casting the scene may have had in mind. Gorill eventually learnt his part, though words and sense suffered lapses. "He hath played on his prologue like a child on a receiver," he persisted in saying, it being long before the time when the recorder was a familiar article of school

51

apparatus and Gorill possibly having the wireless in mind, just about coming into general use. "I am weary of this moon; would he would change": Gorill in turn laid emphasis on every word of the second clause of this, except the right one. "Would he would change—on a receiver," I used to tease Gorill by singing, fitting the words to a song of the day called "Shepherd of the Hills".

A more serious episode in the works of the Bard came to be done later. Just after my brother joined the school the Headmaster enlisted a visiting master to give elocution lessons as an "extra." They could with advantage have been an unoptional part of the curriculum: the Headmaster (who himself came from Oxfordshire) often complained at morning assembly about his pupils' characteristically Fylde lack of aspirates and articulatory lip movements. "Let it come *out*, boys," he would say, opening and shutting his fingers at the side of his mouth to indicate the sort of action required. "Don't mumble"—enunciating the last word with special clarity. A phrase, perhaps a quotation, he often used to illustrate the lamentable sort of speech to be heard was: "Two men sat in a light'ouse, rubbing their 'orny 'ands." Now I have pondered the matter it seems to be that it may have been through the Headmaster's often alarming use of "Master" that I first became aware that I myself used the short "a" and before I left school changed my usage, for in my last year I now recall imitating one of the maids saying at supper time: " 'ere's yer coker (cocoa), Master Fuller." The visiting elocution specialist also lent a hand with the official concert. He had been an actor, Shakespearean it was said (perhaps a Bensonian), now retired or "resting" in the vicinity. His name was Rider Boys; his unromantic rotundity counteracted to some degree by a black velvet jacket and silvery curling hair worn long for those days of the twenties.

Tickets for the concert were printed and cost half a crown, a tidy sum at the time. Boys were encouraged to sell tickets, boarders being limited in this activity since they were only let out of school premises on Saturday evenings, a couple of hours devoted mainly to consuming and stocking up with food. A favoured nearby sweetshop was run by Mr. and Mrs. Waddicor. I believe it was my brother himself who tried to involve Mr. Waddicor in buying a ticket, perhaps two. Mr. Waddicor read the offered pasteboard:

THE BOYS OF SEAFOLDE HOUSE
ASSISTED BY RIDER BOYS . . .

"Who are the *rider* boys?" he asked quite interestedly, probably envisaging a turn of juvenile cyclists or even horsemen.

Under Rider Boys's coaching, and I expect at his suggestion, the potion scene from *Romeo and Juliet* was included in the concert for which Mr. Waddicor's patronage had been sought. My brother, who despite his immature age had already made his mark on the school, played the Apothecary: the Romeo was a boy I shall call Matley, the name of the character founded on his in *The Ruined Boys*. The elocutionist himself produced, also undertaking a solo item, one of Belloc's "Cautionary Tales" which he announced as being by Hilaire Bellòc—a

53

pronunciation whose eccentricity caught my and my brother's fancy, though I suppose it may have had authority in view of the poet's Frog ancestry.

Matley was not in doubt that his destiny was to be a member of the Anglican clergy, High Church wing, but he was also greatly taken with acting, perhaps visualising moving from one career to the other like the Rector of Stiffkey, quite soon to become notorious. At school he was able to combine these two strands of his ambition by dressing as a priest in the dormitory and administering the Sacrament to himself at an altar mainly ornamented by a brass crucifix which could then be bought at Woolworths, possibly still for the sixpence that originally was the price limit ruling in the store. Bespectacled (small oval lenses, gold-rimmed), with stiff, blond, rather frizzy hair (not awfully manageable even with the quantities of Pears' or Californian Poppy solid brilliantine fashionable among the boarders and which the exertions of Saturday evening shopping caused to run in a green veil down their foreheads, particularly the villainously low one of Ames), a pale soft skin and somewhat deficient in chin, he was not the ideal Romeo. And when he removed his spectacles (as he did, of course, to play the part), the naked eye-sockets gave him the air of a white mouse—perhaps the whites of the light-blue eyes were pinkish. However, on the night of the concert make-up offset some of these deficiencies and his success was generally admitted, though some thought he over-acted insufferably. Certainly my brother was a notable, if dwarfish, apothecary.

After the War, my brother stayed on in the forces for

several years, seduced by the promise of rapid promotion in a branch relevant to his pre-war career. On a station to which he was appointed, in a far part of the shrinking Empire, the C of E chaplain turned out to be—who else?—the Reverend David Matley. The character presented was far from the precociously devout dormitory friar, even the unwarrantably narcissistic juvenile lead—much more a one-of-the-boys padre, with a liking for gin-and-tonics, and exuding the raffish tone of some services character from Waugh or Powell. My brother saw quite a bit of him, delighted, as in the case of Hamlet, to find a bizarre but not wholly unpredictable development of personality; confirmatory, too, of my brother's concept of humanity. Alas, again like Hamlet, Matley died at quite an early age.

In the latter years of my time at boarding school my mother, brother and I lived in a "private hotel". I do not know whether, besides my mother's restlessness, there was any reason for our moving from the "rooms" in Miss Barraclough's house, though it is true the accommodation and service provided there were by no means top notch. My mother bought our food, so that little could go wrong with such things as cold ham or even breakfast bacon. I cannot recall the standard of the more elaborate parts of the cuisine: possibly tasty enough, despite the pungent aroma of the kitchen quarters, caused by Miss Barraclough never bathing and intensified by her sleeping there, habits previously referred to. She was helped by the maid, Amy, who had a glide in her eye, her spectacles steel-rimmed and round (anticipating a fashion of today), frizzy-haired (not, like Matley, blond, but black, slightly grizzled). Yet Amy was attractive because of expressive features and a truly kind nature. In those days I thought of myself as a cartoonist in embryo and I especially admired Tom Webster of the *Daily Mail* both for his draughtsmanship and creation of character, human and equine. Buying a comic one evening, I spied the new issue of *Tom Webster's Annual* and craved it. Back at Miss Barraclough's I told Amy of this desirable collection and at once she forked out a shilling (or more likely one and three) so that I could buy it, which I did at once. Even then I felt guilty at using her money, so hard-earned and (I guess) so meagre in amount; nor did the pretence stand up that she too would get a graphic frisson from the booklet. As I write this it comes to me for the first time that not only was Amy a sterling soul: possibly she also loved me, a benefaction that throughout life my character has not counted on. I wonder as well whether my mother learned of the incident (I seem to think she did) and if so very probably she refunded the one and thruppence—for in those days my mother had a reputation for being "soft" (though simple justice rather than sentimental generosity would have seen Amy right).

The private hotel was called Seacliffe and though in that part of the town cliffs had long since given way to concrete it actually overlooked the sea and also Black-pool's then premier hotel, the Metropole. It was owned and run by a lady (whether a widow or *femme sole* perhaps I never knew) with three nubile daughters whose agreeable looks added to the establishment's attractions. Their characters were as contrasted as Chekhov's three girls but their yearnings were not in the least intellectual or towards the metropolis. Our family life, particularly my mother's and particularly in winter when we might be the only guests, became bound up in theirs; and in the season we were involved with a succession of holiday makers, some making departures and reappearances also reminiscent of Chekhov. My brother and I naturally identified, discussed and imitated the more Chekhovian visitors (if degrees are possible with such an epithet). The invariable remark of Mr. Heaton, an elderly vale-tudinarian, I still come out with at appropriate times: "I like a bit of sweet cake with my cup of tea." His liking was in despite of a digestion which incessantly generated wind, expelled through almost closed lips with a noise that began with the labial tenuis and ended with a hiss, no doubt in the hope of disguising its eructatory origin. The reproduction by my brother and me of this curious sound became somewhat obsessive. When I wanted a name for the Asian barrister in my novel *The Father's Comedy* I went back fifty years and simply changed the first letter of the name of the dapper young Indian who had found an unlikely way to Seacliffe, possibly hearing in some sodality of the three sisters' charms. I rather think he was an Oxbridge undergraduate: that and his colour, rare in the provinces at that time, impressed him on us. Did Miss Paine ever come to live at Seacliffe? I have a feeling she did, though without memories of it: she may not have long survived her move from the Hotel Metropole.

The Metropole came to play a part in our lives, albeit for its time and place rather expensive and chic. On the side of it away from the sea was a row of shops, one selling sweets having a notice above it which read: "Princess Marie-Louise, staying at the Hotel Metropole in 1904, said 'Higgins & Co.'s rock is very good' "—or words to that effect, the notice and Higgins & Co. having vanished long since. The hotel lounge, large and of Moorish décor, was available for anyone's use for the price of a drink or a pot of coffee. A small band played there for *thé dansants* as well as background effect in the evenings. On one occasion I recall having pointed out to me the celebrated Dr. Barton, of advanced years but still erect and lean—indeed, skeletal—and an indefatigable dancer, whose habit it was to "stop" the tune being played on his partner's spine as though it were the finger-board of a 'cello, not neglecting to induce an imaginary vibrato. The grillroom, to which access could be gained not only through the hotel but also from the street where stood the emporium of Higgins & Co.—not twenty yards from Seacliffe—served excellent food in a discreet atmosphere of dark wood and starched napery. Probably we got to know Miss Paine through visiting the Metropole lounge. She had a dominating character and a white wig arranged in the close-curled style of Princess Marie-Louise's relative, Queen Mary. I surmise that, for her, living permanently at the Metropole was not achieved without financial difficulty and that this could have been at the root of her running battle with the manager. "Frish" was how Miss Paine pronounced his name (though as my intellectual snobbery developed I imagined it to be really "Frisch"), not prefixing it with "Herr" or even "Mr." More frequently she referred to him as "the Prussian" (memories of the atrocious role, alleged or

58

actual, of that nationality in the late War still vivid), but I do not think he was German—probably, as will appear later, Czech. Sometimes, as I sat over a soft drink among the exotic arches of the lounge with my mother and Miss Paine, "Frish" would be glimpsed in the distance, wearing an outfit similar to that I wore to dancing class, his short light hair and blunt features (Miss Paine's tales of his oppression adding to whatever air of menace he naturally possessed) conforming to one's notions of the essential Germanic nature. (And it is perhaps worth recording that during the 1914–18 War I must have overheard, perhaps read in the newspapers, of German sexual atrocities, for I remember thinking, as an infant, that to have one's bottom—the most sexual part I could conjure up—cut off by a bayonet would inflict utterly unendurable pain as well as present problems of butchery). Yet I divined that Miss Paine was not guiltless in the affairs that set them at daggers drawn. Her part of the grand dame, though plausibly sustained by the wig and a broadly regal style of dress, was threatened by the lack of cash already mentioned and also, I guess, a native closeness. She would sometimes take my brother and me to an early dinner in the Metropole grillroom where, either at her bidding or, more likely, through some subtle appeal to our consciences (mine at least already tenderized by long knowledge of my mother's limited resources after my father's early death) to let her purse down lightly, we almost invariably chose sausages and chips, by far the cheapest dish on the menu. She called the waiters by their first names, especially favouring one with a distinguished grey moustache called John, a

59

refugee from the Bolsheviks according to her: all were deferential though receiving poor monetary benefit, six-pence being about the size of the tips dispensed by her. I seem to remember that on these occasions she herself did not eat or drink: perhaps she had the table d'hôte dinner later in the dining-room, entitled to it as a "resident" under a package deal negotiated with the Prussian, a contract often the subject of complaints from one party or the other. Or maybe her money did not run to a formal evening meal for herself.

What did we talk about over the sausages and chips (usually followed by a vanilla ice, also, by comparison, modestly priced)? Why did Miss Paine entertain those two young boys? Could (it comes to me) my mother have lent her money? Though not lacking a certain zest for experience, I spent much of my childhood (and later life) missing connections in human affairs obvious to others. Possibly such connections embarrassed me or failed to arouse interest, and now time or some censor has deleted them from my memory. At Seacliffe in the early days there stayed a stoutish dapper man of late middle-age called Mr. Wheatcroft. The vee of his waistcoat was edged with white as a result of buttoning in, underneath, two starched linen strips—effective but even then a rare and old-fashioned enhancement of the masculine turn-out. He managed the premier wine merchants of the town, was a friend of Miss Barraclough's brother, was interested in my mother. I see that he could have been over-fond of the bottle, that his marriage might have broken up or his wife been dead, and that it could have been him who had introduced us to Seacliffe. At the time

I would have put from my mind the question of our precise relations with him (it would have embarrassed me to have discovered anything non-superficial), just as I would have taken avoiding action, if at all possible, on seeing any family acquaintance in the street.

Writing these pages the strange question has arisen of motivation in pre-adolescent days, the sources of the strength of one's hold on life. Thinking of animal parallels (coming back to my desk after throwing bread to garden birds, some familiar individuals having been patiently watching me through the study window), one turns, of course, to food. At once I remember, following my father's death—indeed, soon after that cataclysm, for we had still not moved from the house in Waterhead—burst pipes revealed by a thaw, water actually coming down the stairs, myself having a kitchen tea with the servants and, left alone in the confusion, cutting more bread and butter and loading it extravagantly with Tate & Lyle's golden syrup—death, burst pipes, damaged carpets of less consequence than the good bread and my greed. The bread was probably home-baked, as in my maternal grandparents' house, though shop bread (a matter of apology for my grandmother to have to send out for) could also be excellent in those days, and continued to be for years, for I remember well the cylindrical milk loaves, and the small cottage loaves we called "cobs", that were bought from the bakers' shop actually in the same street as Miss Barraclough's house.

I daresay at Seacliffe the food, though of greater formality, was essentially no better than at Miss Barraclough's. The sausages and chips of the Metropole certainly stand out in that epoch. And the only specific memory I have of Seacliffe food is a pudding, regularly on the menu, that pleased me aesthetically as well as being decently edible—half a tinned apricot on a slice of sponge cake, cream poured over. The simulation was of an egg on toast, though it always bothered me that the cream had to be scraped off the fruit before the similitude was fully apparent, in my experience an operation rarely performed by Seacliffe guests.

Food played a great part in life at school, as already implied. There was never enough, except at Sunday lunchtime when one's teeth were furred and appetite jaded through eating, after church, the remains of the sweets bought the previous evening at Waddicor's and elsewhere. Mutton and cabbage and even roast potatoes, almost invariably on the Sunday luncheon menu, I was put off for years after, for under the Headmaster's moral scheme food could not be left on the plate and one had to swallow the nauseating stuff unless it could be hidden in envelope or handkerchief, as narrated in *The Ruined Boys*. Had I to write that book now I would not give it the confident ethics it possesses. The overall plan of the novel is the young hero's gradual discovery during a school year of the moral truth of the school he newly joins (and, incidentally, of the outside world), a truth the reverse of what he first imagines. I would now be more indulgent to the school's deficiencies. To take a small instance: the insufficiency of bread and butter and jam at tea-time, the jam spread ludicrously thin, may have played its part in the modesty of the boarding fee. The values the Headmaster tried to inculcate and the teaching

62

he so ably undertook have lost some of their hypocritical or irrelevant undertones during the decline in public and private standards since the novel was written in the fifties; and my own testy reactionariness has grown. Bullying caused Gorill unhappiness for a time (and I myself suffered similarly) but at least the school made him literate. The order and direction imposed in some respects now seem remarkable: my own tastes were superficially literary yet under the Headmaster, who took the Fifth and Sixth Forms in the subject, I matriculated with distinction in both Mathematics and Additional Mathematics. He owns only a small part of the blame for my entering a profession which called for talents I possessed neither by nature, nor by education thus far. Strangely enough, though the headmaster of *The Ruined Boys* is the villain of the piece, some readers have found him sympathetic, even faintly tragically so.

I left school and was articled to a firm of solicitors when I was sixteen. In preparation for this new life my mother took a flat. One evening, not long after the end of my final term, the door-bell rang and I found the Headmaster standing outside. It was only then, away from the school or school occasions for the first time, that I saw he was shorter than I. Fear or at least unease seized me, though I realised at once I had moved almost entirely out of his power. As a matter of fact there had been an affair in my last or penultimate term that had put me in his bad books and it struck me that he had come to report about that to my mother, belatedness not making this dread speculation much less likely to be true having regard to his measured and steadfast character.

It turned out eventually, after he had chatted to my mother for a while implausibly seated in one of our easy-chairs, that he was inviting me to accompany him to the "Palace Varieties", using my Christian name in making known his intention. For this and other obvious reasons the outing had no connotations of enjoyment, though the theatre, thus colloquially known, usually provided excellent entertainment. It was plainly among the last places one could have associated with the Boss. One sees now that he had acquired two complimentary tickets and lit upon me as (probably last minute) guest because our flat was near the theatre. I cannot think there might have been anything more devious in his great brain. We sat in the dress circle and must have conversed but I recall nothing of what was said.

Top of the bill was Joe Jackson, I suppose one of the funniest music hall mimes ever; I believe Viennese in origin, of Anglo-Austrian parentage, former cycling champion of Austria. In his silent act called, I think, "Stealing a Bicycle" (it would have commended itself to Mr. Waddicor) a dark-chinned tramp in rags came on a woodland stage. A gleaming bicycle is leaning against a tree. After much timid hesitation the tramp tries, with elaborate variations, to ride it away—the rags catch on the cycle, the tyro is also entangled, he and it fall, the machine gradually disintegrates, is wrongly reassembled, and so forth. The deformed vehicle is eventually brilliantly ridden. The Boss did not laugh as the resourceful and hilarious spectacle unfolded, and so I followed suit. In any event I think I would have supposed laughter from me quite *de trop*. I sank my nails into the palms of my hands to suppress the cachinnations that filled my interior like some *question* of the age of torture. Awful pain accompanied incongruously the complete recognition of comic genius. At long last the Headmaster said: "Foolish fellow" and I myself allowed a giggle or two to emerge, as some frightfully strictured patient is blessed by the relief of even a few drops.

# 4.  Happy Valley

While I was a solicitor's articled clerk I met the girl who became my wife. It turned out that she lived quite near Mrs. Vero's and Miss Barraclough's, overlooking an enclosed area of sunken ground near the sea, which perhaps because of subsidence or bog had never been built on and belonged, eventually at any rate, to the municipality. In later days most of it had been laid out as a putting course but in my childhood it was known as "Happy Valley", its main feature being a wooden stage, deckchairs ranged in front, where a pierrot troupe performed. Even when we were only summer visitors to Blackpool I regularly attended this entertainment. So also had my future wife, of course unknown to me—though one speculates as to whether one had not in fact clapped eyes already captivated on the pretty child whose photographs were later examined with Larkinesque interest and emotion.

66

Children were allowed—encouraged—to squat in front of the deckchairs, there being in any case no charge except for the hire of the deckchair, the performers rewarded by a collection and the profits on the sale of copies of the music they sang. So close to the action, so faithful in support, one saw deep into the appearance and characters of the performers as well as learning by heart dialogue spoken, jokes cracked, songs rendered. The make-up on the faces of the actors embrowned the white ruffs they wore, fairly grubby anyway. The soubrette for several seasons was called Lila Dale, a not wholly natural blonde, a little past the first flush of youth, somewhat resembling Alice Faye (to become famous in a few years through the "talkies"). Part of her role in the scheme of things was to get the better of the comedian, whose response to teasing (not utterly unlike Gorill's) was a catchphrase employable in one's own affairs—"Oh you are awful, Lila Dale"—which I still speak with idiosyncratic emphases precisely echoing those used by the oppressed comic. What strange songs became fixed in the mind, sometimes involuntarily returning even sixty years later:

> Avalon, Avalon, nightly I pray:
> Bring back my loved one some day.

Any Arthurian connotation was not grasped by me: I thought of Avalon as being like Dixie—an American place of nostalgic significance. Perhaps I was right. Other pastoral themes did not always concern places: I have already mentioned in Gorillian connection a song that

67

started with the Arnoldian apostrophe "Shepherd of the hills, I hear you calling." And did one really regularly utter, with no sense of the grotesqueness of the claim, "I'm the Sheik of Araby"?—the required pronunciation being "Aŕr-ă-bée" (also "sheik" was then not "shake" but "sheek", conjuring up a less dignified figure). Of course, incongruity of song and singer is inherent in the art form. Býng would sometimes command Gorill to sing for him. Despite the hefty body the voice was thin, uncertain in pitch, strangely high; the song, well-known in a much earlier day, always the same, the tune just discernable:

> Sweetheart, I want to tell you,
> Tell you how much I love you.
> That is the story . . .
> That's all I know now.

The last line, though not part of the song, Gorill fitted to the melody with his Calibanesque lyricism.

I marvel now at the culture with which my mind was stuffed: characters such as Marzipan the Magician from a comic called *The Rainbow*; the vigorous pen and ink illustrations to thé serials in *Chums*; silent films with actors now almost forgotten like George K. Arthur and Lya de Putti, the latter, as he confessed, touching even my grandfather's libido; and songs from drawing-rooms as well as Happy Valley, my mother still being asked to use her mezzo-soprano:

> Dearest, our day is over,
> Ended the dream divine.

You must go back to your life,
I must go back to mine.

—a characteristic song of hers, by Tosti, and which for
my benefit Anthony Powell makes Moreland quote in
*A Dance to the Music of Time*. A wonder that a little
later on there was any room for the *Fantaisie Impromptu*,
*The Dynasts* and so forth.

I also played in a not large, railed-in, public space
over the road from Happy Valley, mostly grass but with
a few flower-beds, which my wife told me later was
known to her as "Sparrow Park". For a reason now
seeming obscure but presumably ornamental, a tall mast
had been erected in the middle of it, sustained by steel
hawsers up which one often tried to climb, though
atrociously rough on the hands. At a certain epoch
Sparrow Park was a not negligible feature of my boyhood,
its sparse, indeed boring, features being of great physical
immediacy—hawsers, rocks in the rockery surrounding
the mast with a peculiarly intense whiteness and sharp-
ness, veronicas in beds dwarfed by the sea winds, the
terminal semicircles on the just-climbable iron railings,
and a worm from its sandy soil, which some larger boy
once tried to make me eat, of predominantly gritty effect.
Most of those I played with there, mainly at a time
before I went to boarding-school, would need, to be
intelligible, explanations too tedious to embark on; the
complexity of even simple lives being an inevitable result
of the lavish time scale involved. Besides, as noted by
Anthony Powell's X. Trapnell, only fiction can be truth-

69

ful in such matters—memory is too defective and distorting.

Mr. Fraser, the man who had been my father's partner (to use the term loosely, for the organisation in the end was that of a private limited liability company) in the rubber-proofing mill between Manchester and Oldham, lived near Sparrow Park, commuting to the mill by train. His presence in Blackpool could well have been an additional reason for my mother coming to live there. For a few years I was friendly with his five children—until their removal to a grander and more distant house, which more or less coincided with my own removal to boarding-school. I will say nothing of this relationship except to recall, by way of introducing a theme possibly felt to be somewhat muted so far, playing with the four sons, perhaps the daughter, too, a fortune-telling game using playing-cards, the object being to ascertain one's matrimonial destiny. First, the cards enabled in some way the girl concerned to be chosen, though restrictions prevailed and one was excited at managing to get a beauty of the neighbourhood, a fragile blonde called Joan Eastwood being greatly in demand; also Cynthia Hall, and in her case the euphonious name alone may have been for me sufficient attraction, for I do not remember her appearance and may well never have seen her. Such was the domination of what Moreland called the "*princesse lointaine* complex" that it did not seem to matter that the girl was known to the chooser merely by sight or reputation. Needless to say, the cards did not reveal my true fate, doubtless at the time in

70

Sparrow Park or Happy Valley, not five hundred yards away.

Other indications of the conjugal ceremony and subsequent life were gained by reciting certain lists to the extent demanded by the card turned up, for example "coach, carriage, something or other, dustcart." I remember pointing out with what seemed masterly sophistry, to alleviate the ill-luck of driving from church in the dustcart, that such a vehicle could be cleaned out and tastefully draped. Freud's childhood "latency period" by no means precludes foolish amatory preoccupations, though true anguish in such areas is reserved for adolescence.

A married sister of Mr. Fraser also lived close to Sparrow Park and I occasionally played with her sons, too. Mr. Fraser's paternal aunt, who had brought up my father and *his* sister as "remittance children" in Caithness, never, so far as I know, came to Blackpool, nor did she marry. She was called Margaret and was known in my family—had probably been thus known to the two siblings in her charge—as "Aunt Maggie". I remember her first at our Waterhead house, to which she paid several visits, presumably from Scotland, my father probably feeling a continuing debt owed to her, for her presence gave him no apparent pleasure, indeed was a source of irritation. She would usually make white puddings during the course of a visit, a delicacy my father was fond of, but their manufacture disordered the house: the operation prolonged, oatmeal and sheep-guts everywhere. There was also a smelly process, perhaps that of boiling the sheep-guts prior to them being used for the

71

pudding skins. I think, too, they presented a problem of procurement, though the oatmeal would come from the sack imported by my father from Scotland and normally used for oatcakes, dipping herrings in before frying or grilling, and his porridge, the last-named eaten with the milk in a separate bowl, a sensible habit adopted by me at that time, later in desuetude.

That Aunt Maggie doted on my father I expect added to her power of exacerbating him. Even my earliest memories of her involve wildish hair, old-fashioned garb, feyness if not precisely at times being a bit M. She was staying with us when the 1920 Derby was run. The matter was discussed, my father liking a bet as much as speculating in options on the Stock Exchange. Aunt Maggie ignored the favoured horses, pronouncing with visionary power that the winner would be Spion Kop. My father, though scornful of the selection, told her to back it if she was so sure. I do not know whether this was done: unlikely, since she was the last person to be involved in vulgar pleasures or material gain. Spion Kop won at odds of 33–1.

In a very short time after my father's death feyness had become paranoia. The last time I saw her was during a stay with my grandparents in Oldham, very likely during the year of my grandfather's mayoralty, 1924–25. One day, after visiting my father's grave in Failsworth Cemetery, we called on Aunt Maggie in her lodgings not very far from the cemetery, nor indeed from the house where I had been born. An allowance was paid to her by Mr. Fraser and at some date she had come permanently down from Scotland. Her lodgings (in fact, one ground-floor room) were also within easy reach of the rubber-proofing mill and hence of her nephew. A brass bedstead dominated the room and Aunt Maggie was in the bed, in grubby white nightgown. Could she even then have been suffering from her terminal illness? I do not know. She had on occasion to get out of bed, for one thing to serve us, from the bag, with shop cakes of a garish kind, utterly despised in my mother's scheme of things and afterwards educed by her as evidence of Aunt Maggie's characteristic improvidence. Aunt Maggie must have been warned of our coming, though neither plates nor beverages were supplied. I was struck by her dirty feet; perhaps as much as by her constantly returning to the theme of being watched by detectives through the window which, where not masked by a dressing-table, looked out on the shabby street. She referred openly and often to my father's death, especially distressing to me who even at that early age wanted such things swept under the carpet, dominated as I was by self-consciousness, an inability to comfort even by a formula of words, a general desire for cosy happiness to reign. "Och, the dear," was a Doric phrase of her lament, still vividly remembered, as is her emphasising the loss of his physical beauty and embarrassingly demonstrating her recognition of its inheritance by my brother and me. Not long after this she died of the malady that had killed him. The undoubtedly painful and squalid circumstances of her end I tried not to dwell on.

Even in the couple of years or so since we had left Oldham my father's grave had, to my mother's distress, become wildly overgrown, despite her having paid for its

73

upkeep. She had had it marked by a large dark-grey marble gravestone, which referred to its containing also the bodies of my infant siblings George and Eric. That they were already there probably accounted for my father being buried in Failsworth, quite a distance from the house in Waterhead where he died. The legend of these deaths, incised so permanently and publicly, impressed me greatly. I saw the marble only once more, though I do not entirely rule out the possibility of again seeking it out, despite the growing toughness, even cynicism, in such areas since those days of loss. I think, too, of the miniature and more commonplace tablet marking my mother in the gardens of a Yorkshire crematorium, never revisited. "Why does my pen not drop from my hand on approaching the infinite pity and tragedy of all the past? It does, poor helpless pen, with what it meets of the ineffable, what it meets of the cold Medusa-face of life, of all the life *lived*, on every side." The conclusion of that wonderful cemeterial passage in Henry James's *Notebooks* comes to mind, but I transcribe it only to underline how far short of what I wished, in art as well as in feeling, I have fallen in life.

I now regret a little that I took so much of my memory of my mother's family for my novel *The Perfect Fool*, not a satisfactory work. It might have been more effective as unadorned autobiography but it would not be sensible to filter out all the actuality from its considerable fictionalising. Something may be said, however, about the greater complications of reality in the matter of my grandparents' children, especially since my fiction has

74

avoided difficulty in such matters, often conveniently positing the orphan or the only child.

My mother's eldest brother, Herbert, died as a young man in the influenza epidemic at the end of the First World War. He had a hare-lip, partly hidden by a moustache with waxed ends on the lines of my grandfather's as I knew it in earliest days (the wax and some of the Nietzschean luxuriance subsequently disappeared in my grandfather's case). At his death Uncle Herbert was married, with an infant daughter: his young widow had to go back to mill work. She bore the same Christian name as my mother and like her had a strong, true singing voice. Probably Herbert had met her in the church choir. The contrasting widowhoods of the two Nellies struck me even as a small boy: my mother, not rich but never in peril of having to try to earn a living; Herbert's widow bringing up my cousin in a small terrace house which perhaps was her parents' house to which she had been forced to return. I forget what Herbert's work was: besides singing, his leisure was occupied with painting. A respectable oil of his of tall grey tree trunks always hung in my grandparents' dining-room, though Herbert's initials were followed by an acknowledgement to some other painter. I was in my grandparents' house when two or three days before his death in 1918 he called on his way home from work saying he wouldn't come in because of a cold.

Two daughters were senior to Herbert: Edith and my mother. Edith, the elder, was known in the family as "Keck", indicating her bossiness as a child. The word is dialect, probably obsolescent even in Edith's youth.

Smaller and fairer than my mother, she had inherited more of my grandfather's characteristics. (My grandmother I see now as a saintly person—not at all pious or lacking in the critical faculty, but simply "good". In my mother the critical side was more apparent, especially in later life, but the "goodness" was not lost and I detect it among my own descendants). Keck was married to the manager of a gas-works and they had a house or flat on the premises. I remember looking down on a courtyard, its cobbles glistening with the dampness common in Oldham, scene of the rats that infested the gas-works marching in military formation in one of their frequent anabases, as sensationally narrated by Uncle Tom, Keck's husband. A somewhat Victorian deathrate persisted in places like Oldham: Keck, too, became a youngish widow. The means she inherited were between my mother's and the other Nellie's, but in some way she eventually met a musician and married him. I say "in some way" because I think Keck was the only one of my maternal uncles and aunts not impressing my youthful mind as musical—though as I write that a memory rises of her "dressing-up" in male attire with my mother, presumably to sing a comic duet. My mother dressed up (the character sometimes favoured being Charlie Chaplin) as late as Seacliffe days: the occasions were rare, the clothes and make-up quite elaborate, the effect successful to others, to me, typically, more or less embarrassing. I suppose my mother's slimness ensured an appeal to the taste prevalent in that ambiguous area; the counterpart of Violet, a character soon to be touched on.

Keck's new husband, youngish, quiet and charming,

with the Wodehousian name of Archie Gladman, was really a trombonist but because of a tendency to TB was forced in the end to play his second instrument, the double-bass, for which there was less demand in the theatre and cinema bands he played in. The coming of the talkies also caused difficulties. Around that epoch he died of the disease mentioned and once more Keck, and her cinema-baffled daughter by Uncle Tom, were left in far from easy circumstances.

One must be struck, setting down such brief lives, by their suitability for the fiction of, say, Arnold Bennett's best period—their illustration of the petty bourgeoisie's social mobility coupled with its immersion in the more or less sordid details of human existence, yet with a readiness to cope with life's material side and in many ways—some the ways of art—to rise above it. John, the sibling immediately following my mother, spent most of his Army service in the First World War in a concert party. He was then extremely young, blond, blue-eyed, slender, and, among other roles, was a "female impersonator", apparently celebrated, for I have a printed postcard of him in drag, signed by him with his sobriquet "Violet". He brought back from the Near East an inscribed cigarette-case presented to him by some local potentate appreciative of his performance. Nothing untoward need be read into this: soon after the War Uncle John married a girl called Edith—I think in fact a sweetheart before he went off to play Violet for the soldiers and the "sheeks"—and lived happily ever after. Never rounded, Edith after bearing her first child lost a fair amount of weight and so was known ever after as

"Bone", a nickname deriving from the communist medico Dr. Edith Bone, at that time, as she was much later, prominent in the news. This also helped to distinguish her, in conversational reference, from "Keck".

Uncle John worked on the administrative side of the cotton trade but as the years went by he did more and more acting for the BBC, appearing, for instance, in a long-running radio series with Wilfred Pickles, and in more serious productions by Norman Swallow and D.G. Bridson. When I was a boy I had seen and admired him in amateur dramatics. In private life he had a professional's power of mimicry and assuming accents; also he could make one laugh. He was close to my grandmother and, like her, "good". He retained remarkably the appearance that had made his personation as Violet so effective. I say this though I did not see him during the last twenty years of his life. In his latter days, after Bone had died and he was permanently in a guest-house aptly, one hopes, called "The Anchorage", on the Fylde coast only a few miles from my school of former times, we corresponded, perhaps his first letter prompted by my election as Oxford's Professor of Poetry. He told me that one of his fellow "guests" at The Anchorage was a Miss Kenworthy, aged eighty-five, who as a young woman had lived in my birthplace, Failsworth, and was acquainted with my father before he was married.

Miss Kenworthy apparently knew my work as a writer before Uncle John tied up at The Anchorage and so was somewhat staggered by the perspectives opened up by his relating his history. He asked me to write to her as an action that would give her pleasure, and a letter came in reply which I will reproduce with certain omissions and explanations—not, however, distorting the facts. I should emphasise that the mystery of my father's origins was pervasive, the veil lifted only in a few accidental ways. For instance, after he had left school my brother went to teach in a prep school while brooding over possible careers and found that the matron had come from Lybster, where Aunt Maggie had reared my father and his sister, and was able to shed some light, also cast a few more shadows. The enigma was deepened by my father's looks and ability. Miss Kenworthy told Uncle John that when he arrived in Failsworth they thought him the scion of Spanish nobility, though it must be said that rickets and poverty made it easy to stand out physically in those days, and later, among the indigenous population of the Manchester conurbation. However, Uncle John confirmed that he looked the hidalgo part, was one of the handsomest men he had known.

*Your letter [wrote Miss Kenworthy on 28 January 1970] revived a lot of old memories. Days spent in my youth in Hollinwood [where the rubber-proofing mill was situated] and Failsworth. I remember Mr. Fraser bringing your father and his sister Minnie, who became a nurse, from Scotland to stay with him in Failsworth. Your father entered the business during the [First] War and evidently made good. I was sorry to hear of his death, also your mother's. I have lost touch with the Frasers, except Mr. Fraser's sister, who is living near Windsor where her younger son lives. She was engaged to my cousin, Dr. Lomas, when they were*

79

*young but he died at twenty-six. Afterwards she mar-*
*ried Dr. Buckley, but it ended in divorce. They had*
*two sons, the elder killed in the [Second, of course]*
*War. It is a small world. I never thought I should*
*know your uncle. I believe Mr. Fraser's father was*
*gamekeeper on some estate in Scotland. Mr. Fraser*
*used to talk about the boy and girl with whom he and*
*his sister played when young. Well it certainly has*
*revived old memories. I am not much good at writing.*
*I am past it. Wishing you every success.*

There was already something amiss with Mrs. Buckley's marriage in the days when I played in Sparrow
Park with her elder little boy (so unlucky in the war in
which I myself had a comparative joy-ride). And was
death rather than desertion put about as the reason for
Dr. Buckley's absence? Perhaps that is exaggerating the
horror of scandal still prevalent in that society at that
time: more likely that, as ever, my understanding was
deficient.

I have left in simplified form the mechanics of my
father's business association with Mr. Fraser and indeed
many details necessarily remain obscure. I will not say
more except that the firm name originally included that
of an elderly Jew who I think had died or retired by the
time my father had achieved partnership (more properly
by then, directorial) status. I mention this for several
reasons. My father was sometimes thought to look not
Spanish but Jewish, an expected presence in a trade in
which in Manchester Jews played a great part. This
may well have been the cause of my grandfather's initial

prejudice against him as a suitor for his younger daughter, especially having regard to my grandfather's familiarity with *The Merchant of Venice*. Some of my father and mother's friends were comfortably-off Jews and I daresay that bore upon the increasing luxury and sophistication of my parents' houses and possessions. The truly intellectual side of Jewish life I suspect did not exist among the Weinbergs and the Gotliffs, friends whose names seem utterly familiar sixty years on, and so was not communicated, but whisky and good cigars, solid furniture, a love of the theatre and of motor cars, an excellent tailor in Manchester memorably called Macbeth, serious bridge—many such things were probably rooted in my father through his Jewish contacts, though the native ground was obviously fertile. I should add also, for there is some evidence for it, that my father's mysterious father may in truth have been Jewish.

My mother, whose cultural background was small-town Tory politics, low Church of England, church choir, parlour music and a general life-style of enforced modesty, had some adjustments to make. She once told me of her astonishment, threat of uncontrollable giggles, when first dining with the Weinbergs (or the Gotliffs) and a preliminary prayer was said, at my father, not having a skull-cap (yarmulke) like the other males, putting his folded napkin on his head. After his death she more or less slowly regressed to the styles and prejudices of her upbringing, though she was always lavish about her clothes and saw that my first suit with long trousers was made to measure, also finding a decent tailors and outfitters in Blackpool called Southworths, who supplied my suits and overcoats until I left the town when I was twenty-three or twenty-four.

My father's pleasure in going to the theatre may well have been useful common ground during any sticky times with my grandfather during his courtship of my mother. I believe I myself saw the comedian Wilkie Bard in a pantomime to which I was taken by my parents in extreme youth, but I cannot be sure, so rapidly and vividly did a passage from the production in question become a part of what Carlyle in his *Reminiscences* reminds us the Germans call (or used to call) *Coterie-sprache*—family-circle dialect. Wilkie Bard in the person of Simple Simon is granted three wishes by the Fairy Godmother. When she is gone he expresses his desire—in his eagerness to test out his good fortune, a modest but eccentric one: "I wish I was a hard-boiled egg." His eyes tight shut, he asks the audience: "Is it doing it?" Both phrases came to be applied in a variety of family contexts. Wilkie Bard also originated one of my grandfather's sayings, plainly at a much earlier stage of the comedian's career, and I remember my grandfather once explaining the ambient theatrical circumstances. Wilkie Bard has quarrelled with his stooge and they are to fight. Bard lays down the rules: "When I say 'Begin', begin. When I say 'Leave off', leave off." They face up. Bard says "Begin", strikes a blow, then immediately says "Leave off." *Da capo*. Possibly Wilkie Bard is not much remembered today. His most famous song ended "I'd like to sing in opera, sing in opera, sing in op-pop-pop-pop-era."

I called Mr. Fraser "Uncle Alf", in the manner of the

North. His mode of life may too have caught something from Jewish business associates. After he had moved from the Happy Valley area we were only very occasional visitors. In the drawing-room of the new house was a grand piano, a pianola of such sophistication that as indications came round on the roll—"*p*", say, or "*rall*"—a row of levers in front of the keyboard enabled one to add the required expressiveness. The piano rolls available included classical pieces so one temporarily became a Tregenza of the instrument. Typical of my lack of enterprise that I never even attempted to learn the piano. I decided at an early age that it was something I could not do, just as having established myself as open sprint champion as early as my penultimate year at school I never tried to win the half mile or mile.

On one visit to the Frasers' I accidentally came across Uncle Alf in a room lit only by a lamp that threw illumination on his open book, a drink at his side. The comfort and purpose of the scene caught my admiration. Perhaps he was turning a page with the hand on which, from a cause never revealed, one finger lacked its top joint. The minaciousness of this feature was recalled later by the sudden staggering close-up of the hand of the Godfrey Tearle character in Hitchcock's *The Thirty-nine Steps*. The rubber-proofing mill had obviously continued to prosper. It was sometimes said in my family that my mother's shares had been acquired by Uncle Alf too cheaply. Was it a trace of guilt or mere respect for culture that prompted him at the end of my schooldays to enquire about my taste in gramophone records apropos of a birthday present? More probably my fascination with the pianola had tickled him, glad to have an enthusiast for his extravagance—though I expect I was too green ever to have discussed music with him. A list was sent and to my amazement he bought everything on it. Included were Bax's *Tintagel* and some Bach violin sonatas played by Isolde Menges and Harold Samuel, somewhat odd indication of breadth of taste, still persisting. Jewish generosity and ostentation unfortunately played little part in my own life, the petty-bourgeois anal-erotic character pretty well taking over.

A Gentile friendship, however, best survived the crisis of my father's death; a couple addressed by my brother and me as Uncle Fred and Auntie Vi, the titles again honorific. Uncle Fred had been a business associate, a drysalter; and he also took his family for holidays on the Fylde coast, eventually retiring there. I remember him from my father's lifetime: he owned an unusual car—a Ford with an English body, however that had come about. I was in it once when he drove in the tram track leading from Blackpool to St. Annes (where The Anchorage was situated in later times) and took the speedometer up to what seemed then the dashing speed of 30 mph. He called to my father, also driving an open car nearby (could it have been his first car, the Yankee Overland?): "I'm a tram." It comes to me that Uncle Fred, small, sandy, humorous, was no stranger to the bottle, certainly in retirement, though that epoch was sadly truncated for I judge him to have been no more than fiftyish when he died—leaving £30,000, a tidy sum for the twenties.

His ménage in the house on the front at Lytham where he ended his days had a good few features regarded by my brother and me as bizarre. It included at one time both Vi's parents, the father already decrepit. I once came into a room where he was sitting with eyes closed, head forward, a thread of saliva hanging from his open mouth, and with a lurch of the stomach thought he was dead. On that occasion he had merely fallen asleep. Vi's mother survived him but most of the time I knew her was suffering from the effects of a stroke, though capable of being inserted into the large, chauffeured limousine Uncle Fred possessed at that period, for a "drive". She was troubled by one of her toes, which gradually stuck up to such an extent as to stop her getting a shoe on. The solution adopted, striking as it seemed to me, was to have the toe amputated. I would guess this proposed and arranged by Auntie Vi, always sweepingly direct and practical. My mother told me of being with her when buying gramophone records. "Yes, I'll have that," she would repeatedly say after a few revolutions of the disc played by the shop assistant, carrying into everyday occasions Uncle Alf's birthday lavishness.

This was the heyday of the coloured duetists, Layton and Johnstone (the former only recently dead, well into his eighties), a liking for whose records Vi passed on to my mother. From these, as from Lila Dale and her confrères, I got to know many songs including one I sang then as incongruously as "The Sheik of Araby" but which today becomes more and more apt:

> There's nothing left for me,
> Of days that used to be,
> They're just a memory among my souvenirs.

From my mother, herself an excellent if limited cook, I inherited a notebook of recipes, unfortunately sparse and unsystematic. However, it includes some of Auntie Vi's recipes which in their generous proportions of rich to plain ingredients reflect her nature, and fondness for what she conceived to be the good things of life, e.g:

## PLUM CAKE (VI)

6 oz. butter, 2 oz. syrup, 6 oz. caster sugar.
Beat these to a cream, add 3 eggs and ¼pt. warm milk, and beat again.
Add ½lb. [plain?] flour, ½ teaspoon baking powder, 1lb. currants, ¼lb. candied peel, 3 oz. ground almonds.
[No oven temperature or baking time given, but presumably lowish and prolonged respectively.]

Discussion among Fred and Vi's friends was caused by the rise in the household of a Rasputin figure—the comparison is purely metaphorical—called Mr. Marple who I believe began as the person in charge of Uncle Fred's motor yacht. When I was aboard, this commodious vessel merely chugged about the Ribble estuary—to my relief, for I feared the open sea, with its twin threat of sickness and death by drowning. But longer voyages were undertaken, though these did not satisfy Mr. Marple's capabilities, and gradually he came to participate in most family affairs, even appearing in the drawing-room at teatime, and probably giving advice over such problems as the vertical toe. He was certainly useful in getting the great bulk of Vi's mother into the back of the limousine, but the attractions of his physique and conversation seemed minimal, complacency and dogma ruling in the latter area.

Who can tell from the outside what forces operate within a family, particularly where cash or infatuation plays a covert part? When Uncle Fred died some thought that Mr. Marple would succeed in marrying Auntie Vi, but both the yacht and its Palinurus were got rid of (with what complexities I do not know) and she settled down to widowhood. She would have been an attractive catch and not only for her money: pretty, blonde, plumpish, with fine pale skin, she was always enclosed in a cloud of Caron's Sweet Pea, and she managed her household with controlled lavishness. Perhaps she had gone along too easily with Fred's whims and eccentricities: once on a country drive their little daughter, an only child, had coveted a lamb seen on a farm. This was bought for her more or less on the spot and actually kept in the house until its droppings became too copious to tolerate. But to have stood out against Fred in such matters would have implied an element of feminine nagging quite alien to her nature. Indeed, who knows but what she was the prime mover in the lamb affair?

All these older people mentioned are dead to my knowledge or must surely be dead, but as I write this in the Spring of 1978 my grandparents' youngest child, called Fred after his father, lives still. We exchange an occasional letter but I have not seen him for a great many years. He is not all that much older than me: when I was born he went off to school gleefully repeating "I'm an uncle." He was still living with my grandparents well on into my boyhood, the source of a few miscellaneous precepts in the conduct of life I would never have thought to challenge though incapable of following them myself; for example, that in handwriting the movement of the pen must be guided by the whole hand not just the fingers. Though at the time of this pronouncement he was studying for some technical qualification in the grocery trade, in the end he succeeded my grandfather as Superintendent Registrar of Births, Marriages and Deaths where penmanship was more to the point—at any rate in the time of my grandfather who I remember making the register entries and writing the certificates in his copperplate hand (two fingers extended on top of the pen, the other two, victims of the contracture previously mentioned, tucked neatly away). The boxes of fine pen-nibs, capable of meticulous thickening of the down-strokes nonetheless; the miniature pair of clogs; the wooden bas-relief by some primitive artist of a Millet-esque man with a wheelbarrow—such memorabilia of visits to my grandfather's office must have descended to Uncle Freddy with the job. The office was near Tommyfield, Oldham's ancient open marketplace where once were to be found such figures in my grandfather's lore as the man standing there (as he would say on 31 December) with as many noses as there are days in the year, and the vendor of ice-cream who called: "It's made from milk, sugar and eggs; highly flavoured with the juice of the pine; frozen into consistency by the power of ice, assisted by muriated soda. Only one half-penny a glass." Those, of course, were the days when the results of even Auntie Vi's kind of recipes might be found in the market.

Perhaps from Uncle Freddy came my admiration for pier-end music, to be undermined at school though perhaps never entirely deleted—composers such as Luigini and Eric Coates played by him on my grandparents' gramophone, exotically single-horned like a fabulous beast. I must add, however, that all his life he has sung more serious music with choral societies, including that of the BBC. Alas, the Broadbentian vocal powers were not part of my inheritance: "Avalon" and "Shepherd of the Hills" and "Parted" have down the years been warbled by me more in Gorill's style.

# 5.   The Metropole

*The wind attendant on the solstices*
*Blows on the shutters of the metropoles,*
*Stirring no poet in his sleep, and tolls*
*The grand idea of the villages.*
                                        Wallace Stevens

---

For a reason I never knew or have forgotten, phrase applicable to much of these reminiscences, the proprietress and her three daughters left Seacliffe. Perhaps the lease was up or she sold the business. We went with them to a like establishment farther north in the town, only obliquely overlooking the sea, the house smaller, more elegant, only recently—possibly at that moment—having changed from use as a private residence. Here I passed the holidays of my later schooldays: dim period, scarcely worth trying in the least to depict, as it seems to me now. Where were the inspiriting forces that worked on other poets in their youth? "Ugliness be thou my beauty," I might have said to myself at almost every
90

stage of my life, but in Blackpool I had lost the scenes of early childhood, meaningful however banal—the mill chimneys, red brick both newish and grimy, muddy cobbles wisped with cotton escaped from great sacks on horse-drawn carts, winter days whose atmosphere was so heavily yellowish-gray that they never really grew light, shawled women and girls, trams redolent of workers' dinners carried in white basins closed with white-spotted red cotton handerchiefs and where one sat on yellow-varnished, hole-ventilated wooden seats facing passengers often bow-legged, usually pale. This was a spiritual loss, felt quite early (no doubt subconsciously connected with my lost father), and therefore significant to me as the writer I wanted from the age of fifteen or so to become. The Pennine green fields and small dark-grey valley towns, mostly known from our tragically few years at Waterhead, came rather into the category of dream landscapes—desirable things theoretically available yet never satisfactorily appreciated let alone possessed. Some imp of the perverse has kept me from what I know I would have responded to warmly in this area, just as I never fulfilled my love of billiards and snooker nor, like Proust, got to Venice. Not until 1955 did I even have a garden of my own. As a youth I was only exiguously attended by a vision splendid.

I also seemed handicapped as a novelist by leaving the speech and social life of industrial east Lancashire at so early an age. The whining, frozen-lipped tones of Blackpool which the Boss tried to eradicate in his pupils were perhaps the dilute result of various Lancashire and Yorkshire accents brought by those who had come to the

91

holiday town in retirement or to make their modest piles in catering or entertainment. The social strata were simplified; the population much reduced out of season, of course, and to a degree culturally stagnant. In time I did conceive that a broadish novel might be written, possibly on the lines of those American novels located in small towns delineating the old founder families, the smart set, the judge, the bootlegger, and so forth, but I was never quite sufficiently impelled to try to write it. Except insofar as I feel guilt about all books left unwritten, I do not regret the absence of the seaside resort novel, but I believe, given a decade more of Oldham life, I might have attempted a fiction about the work, politics and classes of a northern manufacturing town (which my *Image of a Society* does not aspire to).

I suppose what Blackpool had to offer in the realm of the Wordsworthian made its mark: seabirds, ribbed sand, rugeous sunsets—all appearing at the end of the short street, Wilton Parade, in which the new private hotel was situate. An early poem ends:

They watch a portion of the slaty sea
detach itself, flutter and become a gull,
rise wheeling, crying, over the dissolving pier
whose minarets are charcoaled on the sky.

I say "early" but the poem was probably written in 1932, "they" being poor and exploited fishermen, required type of dramatis personae for poetry of the time. Before that epoch I wrote a fair amount of muck, perhaps some still to be found in one of the trunks in the loft: I doubt if it would contain much as accurate as the image implied by "dissolving" for the pier at high-tide (and for its rusting legs), somewhat surprising and pleasing now. In my last year at school, 1928, or possibly earlier, a typewriter became available (by what mysterious means I do not recall) and I typed out some short stories in the manner of H.G. Wells and Aldous Huxley and sent them to periodicals, never neglecting to add in the covering letter some such smarm as "The fact that I am sixteen may be useful for publicity purposes", rather in the manner of "E.J. Thribb (17)". My tyro's one-finger typing in single spacing would have helped to ensure rejection, though very early on I was excited to get instead of a rejection slip a letter from the then editor of *John o' London's Weekly,* Wilfred Whitten, in which he conferred a word of praise, adding that I must read authors like Galsworthy for all I was worth so that I would learn both what to include and what to reject in my fiction. Kind action, though at the time I did not see the rejection point, it being difficult enough to get material *in*.

I doubt if my really early work could now be found—a minuscule play, for instance, called *Barabbas,* giving some twist to the crucifixion story that escapes me; and another drama, more appropriately skeletal because in the manner of Maeterlinck. Both in prose. Even these were written at an age which for some writers would be considered advanced, fourteen or perhaps early fifteen (almost every month counted in those days). The latter age I judge to be when I wrote for some purpose not of self-expression (perhaps humour or parody) a short piece of blank verse. As soon as I showed it to a friend I

93

realised it was not blank verse at all but syllabic verse: that is, I had misapprehended until then the stress element in English poetry; or even more gormlessly had known perfectly well what blank verse sounded like but failed to *compris* the method of getting that effect. All the same, my "ear" was plainly never a strong point in my poetic equipment: at any rate·an odd gap existed between ear and pen. As I write this, a longish poem in octosyllabics has just appeared in the magazine *Encounter,* a great many lines of which do not scan at all:

> His talent was just too immense.
> He had to go. There was no choice.
> Like Mozart he was *Heaven*-sent
> And back to *Heaven* he soon went.

Can it be that in fifty years we have regressed to the fifteenth century situation and poets are again baffled by prosody? It may well be that if Auden had not brought traditional metrics back into fashion bafflement would have arrived earlier, myself in danger of contributing.

Apart from a mock Elizabethan song composed as a show-off soon after the blank verse episode I did not write any verse at school, unless some beneficent censor has operated on my recall. I wanted to write prose drama and fiction, mainly the latter. My turning into a poet seems slightly mysterious, out of character: even now, especially with novels behind me, I feel unease at seeing myself referred to as "the poet".

Where precisely did I write *Barabbas* and the like? I kept the MSS in the pockets of those wallet

94

affairs—"compendiums" of stationary, as they were called—conveniently containing writing pad and envelopes, and used by my mother. I remember having these things at my grandparents' house in holiday time but the recollection is lost of sitting down to write in Seacliffe or the house in Wilton Parade. Not that I would have sat down for long. Like some early machine-gun, I have always operated in rapid, short, unreliable bursts. Only in fairly recent years have I ever sufficiently re-drafted. The small lined pads are typical of the feeble materials I used, at any rate for many years. In other words my habits of literary work were—have never really ceased to be—thoroughly bad. When we went on holiday in the later thirties with Julian Symons, actually younger than me, I observed with guilt and awe his professional industry and equipment: knuckling down to work after an arduous evening of paper games; using green paper in the manner (wasn't it?) of Dumas *père*. It is the only advice one can give to the young: work regularly; rewrite; keep a journal, a commonplace book; indulge yourself with pens, notebook, paper, typewriter, for they will inspire when life has failed.

Though at Wilton Parade we spent a good deal of time in the proprietress' sitting-room, it is unlikely I wrote anything there, what with the daughters and the pursuing young men, and so forth. In a corner on a card table was a portable gramophone. The only classical record was of Paderewski playing Liszt's Second Hungarian Rhapsody which I put on a lot, for for at school I was entering the Tregenza era. We did not have our own gramophone either there or at Seacliffe: it must have been sold or

95

given away, together with the stock of records accumulated at Miss Barraclough's during the time of Auntie Vi's musical influence. My mother bought me an HMV portable after we had moved from Wilton Parade to the flat she took when I left school (to which, in our earliest days there, the Boss paid his memorable visit) and I began to accumulate records far from the Layton and Johnstone category. I carried on with a friendship formed at school with a day-boy, one of the two pianists already mentioned, who already had a record collection, from which I learnt such sacred and reverberant names as Otto Klemperer and Karl Muck. Because Leslie greatly admired Cortot he possessed Cèsar Franck's *Variations Symphoniques* played by that pianist but his taste was really more severely classical. I nervously revealed to him my purchase of an album of Ignaz Friedman's performance of the Grieg piano concerto on dark-blue label Columbia discs, the work to a tyro of those days seeming almost modern and possibly ephemeral. A little later I was even more nervous about Ravel's *Introduction and Allegro,* on plum label HMVs, the colour again indicating cheapness. But I must not waffle on about gramophone records, my interest in which has gone on, no less coloured by collector's crankiness.

It was an odd flat for my mother to have rented (though she was not then quite so conventional as she later became). She complained that it was somewhat beyond her means, but in reality she guarded her capital and income rather too carefully, and less for herself than for her sons. The flat, on the second floor of a building whose ground floor was shops, looked out from its sitting-room and main bedroom over the promenade to the sea. It was actually just closer to the centre of the town than the Hotel Metropole, the entrance to which—at the other end to the grillroom meagrely patronised by Miss Paine—could be seen by us diagonally across the road. The flat's bathroom and second bedroom were not behind the, so to speak, front door, but across the access staircase; and the cooking arrangements hidden by a partition and screen in the dining-room. This bohemian lay-out had given my mother food for thought before she signed on the dotted line.

In the couple of years or so that had elapsed since Seacliffe days Miss Paine had disappeared from our lives, possibly dead, but the Prussian was still in charge over the road and seen when I went to the chamber concerts held there a little later which attracted the Blackpool musical èlite, such as it was, and gave me a bit of needed practice in small talk with the posh.

Strangely, at a time when I no longer frequented the Metropole lounge, in house-that-Jack-built fashion I got to know the leader of the tiny hotel orchestra through its pianist, who had married the girl who had been the inseparable friend of my wife-to-be in her school days and after. So I never heard the band when it included these two excellent players, but I sometimes listened to them at the pianist's flat, probably playing the Max Bruch No 1, whose strains even today recall the fiddler, a big shambling fellow who had it not been for his tender phrasing of the Bruch melodies and his committing suicide after his wife's death one would have thought utterly commonplace. Len, the pianist, told me that Frish was no Prussian but a Czech (possibly Sudeten German, soon to become a direly familiar phrase), who regularly requested the orchestra to play the overture to Smetana's most celebrated opera, which he pronounced *The Battered Bride*.

So a fresh set of characters appeared on the scene. Naturally the most vivid were those working in the office of the solicitors, T, & F. Wylie Kay, where I was to serve my five years' articles. I had left school at Christmas 1928 but had to wait until the following February or March to start my service, for the firm chosen was in the upset of moving from long-occupied offices in the town's main professional street to a larger building, in fact opposite the entrance to our new flat, diagonally across a modest-sized square. For this brief journey I remember putting on, certainly at first, a newly-acquired trilby hat, strange symbol of emancipation from the Boss. The overcoat I wore with the hat I must surely have had at school, bought from the ready-made department of the tailors already mentioned, Southworths. But the next overcoat I had, quite soon, was certainly bespoke from them: it was black, with a lighter fleck, and I instructed them to make it long, with a half-belt at the back. With this I wore a black snap-brim trilby. The effect intended was of a literary man; the result more like the spiv character Slasher Green, portrayed by the comedian Sid Field after the Second War. I may add that the last overcoat made to my specification by Southworths, just before I got a job in Kent in 1935 or early 1936, was a complete contrast. The material was expensive: substantial, smooth, camel-coloured. I changed to an all-round
98

belt and the pleats it enclosed were smaller and more numerous than in the Slasher Green article—gathers, almost, It was double-breasted, long, very warm. By 1940 it had seen better days according to the high standards of non-shabbiness inherited from my mother, and I lent it to Giles Romilly when he was sent by his newspaper, the *Mirror,* to cover the Norwegian operations. Unfortunately he was captured by the Germans in that fiasco and being Winston Churchill's nephew was sent to Colditz with other VIP prisoners, so the loan was permanent. Typical of me that I cannot remember asking him, when we met again after the War, if he had found it useful in the rigours of that now well-known fortress.

My brother also patronized Southworths. The man we used to see in the ready-to-wear department was one of two Southworth brothers, extremely lean, hair parted in the middle, greased perhaps with Pears' Solidified, vertical lines in his cheeks through (or causing) a constricted manner of speech, the lips tight at the corners, the words emerging from some minimum labial movement at the centre. He would expertly button the jacket one was trying on, run his finger under the lapels to ensure they were sitting properly, and more often than not remark: "Very tony, Mr Fuller. Extremely nutty." My brother's imitation was good, perhaps facilitated by his past experience as the Apothecary in *Romeo and Juliet.* Both he and I had a fetish for having jackets and overcoats made to fit over-snugly. I had a brown and cream houndstooth Harris tweed jacket I was very fond of: it lasted so long that even I came to see that it should have been cut more generously. Besides, it embodied

99

another quirk of mine that I eventually realised was aesthetically insupportable—double-breasted style lapels on a single-breasted jacket. More successful aesthetically was a pair of dark grey, almost black, flannel trousers I ordered after seeing Charles Sweeney playing in a similar pair in the åmateur golf championship at Royal Lytham St. Annes. Before then flannel trousers had been light grey, the lighter the better. The last garments made for me by Southworths were two suits, just before my marriage in 1936, one of which I wore at the ceremony. Both were light brown—the two materials had been so attractive I could not choose between them and had them both. One cost £3. 10s., the other three guineas.

I was articled to Eric Wylie Kay. He and his uncle, Tom, were the only partners at that time. It was a sound and flourishing family firm. Both Mr. Eric and Mr. Tom were nutty, Eric also handsome in the teeth and toothbrush moustache style of a subaltern of the first war, somewhat later made famous by Anthony Eden. A man from Savile Row used to come and measure Mr. Tom for his suits, which were said to cost fourteen guineas apiece, putting Southworths in proper perspective. T. & F. Wylie Kay was not the right sort of firm to train me in the practice of the law, as will appear. But a harder furrow was of my own rejecting. My mother had been put on to a much smaller firm in Preston where there was a vacancy for an articled clerk—Whittle & Co, the "Co" being then a fiction—and we had gone for an interview. The waiting-room was separated from a clerks' office merely by an obscure-glass partition. From behind this, as we waited to see Mr. Whittle, came the severe Lancashire tones of a buxom, middle-aged, woman managing-clerk, letting some smaller fry have it in no uncertain terms. My blood ran cold at the prospect of a régime as repressive as that of the Boss'. Nor was I warmed by Mr. Whittle, a fairly diminutive cripple with a rubber-tipped stick and incisive voice, who possibly simply to emphasise value for money (in those days a premium had normally to be paid for articles, with no return by way of salary) spoke of the hard and thorough training his office would afford, especially in the unappealing litigation field. Afterwards my mother immediately agreed as to Whittle & Co's unsuitability, for she was as "soft" as I was in such matters. The avoidance of the crunches in life are often within one's own power; but the benefit may be questionable. In the end my career in the law was outwardly more successful than my career in letters, though I was in middle-age before I found scope for such legal talents as I possessed. An early shake-up by Mr. Whittle might have brought that about far earlier. It was even the same in the Navy. An instinct for self-preservation made me put my name down for a mysterious long course while I was still at my initial training establishment. The result was I diverted myself from an executive commission to being an NCO in the mechanics of radar, and it was not until 1944, eventually commissioned and at the Admiralty, that I had (as Technical Assistant to the Director of Naval Air Radio) any sustained usefulness or relief from excruciating boredom.

At T. & F. Wylie Kay's I was put into a topmost room with another articled clerk (who happened to have

101

the same name as Gorill's tormentor, Byng) and the engrossing clerk. The latter worked on a stool at a high sloping "desk" fitted along one wall and evidently brought from the old premises. All the deeds turned out by the firm were still "engrossed" by hand, rather than typed, though "parchment substitute" was sometimes used instead of parchment. The engrossing clerk was a young man called Norman Lees (who later reported the Boss' longevity), shortish, with a large intelligent head and lively features. I shall refer to him by his surname, as was customary in those times. He had done well at his late school and it was an indication of current economic conditions and educational opportunity that he stuck at the soul-destroying job of copying out in copperplate handwriting the typewritten drafts brought into him by the managing clerks and occasionally the partners. One says "copperplate" but though Lees threw off the engrossing clerk's various arts ("texting" the gothic lettering where that was required; "pouncing" the parchment; erasing errors with a penknife or razor-blade and rubbing the erasure smooth with the tip of a (cow?) horn to enable it to be written over; sewing sheets together with green "ferret"; affixing the wax seals with their attendant ribbons; and so forth) compared say with my grandfather he was not a good calligraphist. His finished work had a superficial air of authenticity but closer inspection might reveal letters unjoined or ill-formed, even ambiguous, especially when he had been trying, always in vain, to catch up with his back-log of drafts. The engrossed deeds were sometimes complained about by the conveyancing managing clerk, J.T. Ogden—who was the first of that alas obsolescent breed I got to know and by no means the last I came to regard with respect and admiration, tinged with fear. Not that JTO was ever other than the kindest of men but one's work often failed (and one knew it was going to fail) to measure up to his standards. I greatly admired his fluent handwriting, evolved from a time when he was an engrossing clerk, and his draft deeds, founded on the most traditional of the conveyancing precedent books, *Prideaux*. It was only conscientiousness brought to the point of exacerbation that caused him so often to burst into the attic room, look with angry despair at the draft deeds ranged to Lees's right on the sloping desk, groan, and bring a few of his most urgent ones to the front of the row—a ploy often frustrated by others doing the same.

Lees relished a good many things in life; some surprising, having regard to a background which today might almost be conceived of as "deprived". His mother had died when he and his sister were young: his father, in a by no means lucrative job, had never remarried. He had a good memory for the comic side of his schooldays. Some things he told me I used in novels years afterwards: others I wished I could have worked in, like the parody of Tennyson's "The Revenge", one brilliant line only of which remains with me now:

And a pinnace, like a buttered turd, came sliding from
far away.

I soon discovered that he had a taste for reading as individual as most elements in his make-up. He liked particularly Arnold Bennett's novels and even more the journal that I think began to be published about this

103

time. The latter would appeal partly because of its depiction of a provincial breaking into the world of high politics, art and large yachts, without that provincial ceasing to see through the flummery. Above all, Lees had the sharpest sense of the absurd and the fallible in human behaviour, although his life was conventional, his pleasures largely orthodox. His Saturday nights, for instance, were at this epoch always spent drinking with male companions. But his Monday morning reports rarely failed to single out some strangely memorable features of what might seem invincibly tedious hours. One of his friends, weary of being repetitively interrogated during the evening about a facial wound, wrote out and pinned to his lapel a notice:

## I HAVE CUT MYSELF WHILE SHAVING WITH A POM-POM PENNY BLADE

The resonance of this (apart from its being a "four-teener", as I am sure Lees also appreciated) was the fact that the penny razor-blade, competing with Gillette's product at threepence, was an article whose dubiety (and danger) was significantly reflected in a brand-name such as "Pom-pom". Lees's analysis of all at Wylie Kay's was devastating and led to many running gags between us. There was, too, a deep quirkiness and reticence about him which made him, especially in later life, agreeably unpredictable, forcing one on the *qui vive*.

His power of looking with detachment at the kind of life and culture he had inherited, and which in his engrossing clerk days he still more or less moved in, was

104

remarkable. I remember his once pointing out the grammatical curiousness of the idiom (I think a wholly North of England one) "partly what", and then moving on to a kind of Empsonian discussion (the occasion must have been in a pub) of the difference between saying a glass was "partly what full" and "partly what empty".

Looking back, I see that he in his turn was influenced, possibly his life transformed, by being put in with the articled clerks, passing his days on terms of intellectual equality with them. He was greatly taken by an overcoat belonging to Byng. It should be said that the latter was an Oxbridge graduate and therefore older than me and serving only three years' articles. The overcoat in question, a light-weight tweed, single-breasted with raglan sleeves—a far cry from the Slasher Green garment later made for me—had been built for Byng by obviously excellent tailors in his university town. Lees saw "Raglan", as he always called the coat, as evidence of some superior style in life, not necessarily the result of affluance, more a tradition or *modus operandi* which it was a provincial's (or any supposed inferior's) highest duty to acquire, the end result being a satisfactory, indeed beautiful, conquest of the grosser side of existence. He speculated as to whether the material of which Raglan was made could not be classed as "ratcatcher", a term he had picked up in his reading, maybe apropos of Edward VII or George VI (the earliest slang usage of the word in the Supplement to the OED—the *Field* in 1930—is surely too late and too esoteric). It was some time, I think after my days at Wylie Kay's, before Lees's own turn-out reflected any notion of mastering life, and

105

then merely in the shape of good dark suits or, for leisure, neat tweed jackets and flannel trousers. I remember once battling with him to the trams on the Promenade in one of Blackpool's characteristic squalls of wind and rain—and this must have been well into my articles for we were both bound for South Shore where he lived and where my mother had once more taken "rooms". He wore a bowler hat, necessarily large but of antique block, and his far from new, drab garbardine raincoat was buttoned to the throat. I said fondly to this Dickensian (or, rather, Gissingesque) figure: "The seedy clerk." The phrase as applied, and in such weather, struck me as funny but the reality was probably not so funny, Lees and his family at that time far from comfortably off.

We were eventually joined in the attic room by a third articled clerk whose purchase of an expensive trilby hat made by Stetson (could it actually have been imported from the States?) and other would-be grandiose gestures failed to impress Lees, whose mind as ever was fixed on some style beyond the fashionable or showy. His destiny may be briefly told. After my articles expired and I left Wylie Kay's, the post of engrossing clerk was seen to be anachronistic and Lees became a conveyancing clerk. The job presented no difficulties: quite apart from his ability, he had engrossed and read aloud (to check against the drafts) so many deeds of various kinds he was a walking encyclopaedia of precedents. Later he was given his articles, passed his examinations and qualified as a solicitor, eventually setting up on his own. He became quite famous in the local police and county courts, and his practice prospered. He had married one of the short-hand-typists at Wylie Kay's, the courtship typically kept dark. His two daughters did well educationally, one of them publishing a book with the OUP on A.C. Bradley, a stroke of unobvious gamesmanship Lees no doubt much appreciated: later she was the author of an excellent book on Coleridge. In a strange way everything he achieved, though of conventional success, took on an element of the good or ideal life, the provincial's dream fulfilled. The beer he drank, cigarettes smoked, bridge played, the mass-produced car he drove, golf-club eventually joined: on all these he conferred some proper value of his own; everything to do with the car, for example, carried off in a competent but offhand manner, as though to demonstrate its useful but essentially unBennettesque nature. The first time he visited us in London by car I gave him directions. He told me later that a phrase of these had become a useful family saying: "Eschew all side roads." Who knows what even more ludicrous traits of one's persona he had anatomized?

The articled clerks were idle beyond belief. No wonder Lees lagged in his engrossing. When the third articled clerk arrived we had a bridge four, and with a system of safeguards such as laying dummy out in a desk drawer which could be shut when Ogden *et al* were heard approaching, rubbers were more or less peacefully played. Byng had played at Oxbridge: he was a competent performer. I am not sure about Lees's expertise in the initial stages: he would have rapidly improved, anyway. As for myself, I had watched from an infantile age my parents and grandparents (and possibly even the Weinbergs and Gotliffes) play what was then merely auction

107

bridge. In our Waterhead house when I must have been no more than seven or eight one of a serious four was called from the table and I offered with trepidation to take the hand, successfully carrying off this first excursion into actual play. I have already referred to my father's and grandfather's devotion to the game, the latter playing pretty well every night of his later life at the Conservative Club in Oldham. The underground family complaint was that whisky and bridge losses reduced his always modest income but this can scarcely have been true in any serious sense, though perhaps his rate of saving suffered, was extinguished even. I wonder whether at the club he came out with the patter indulged in at the family bridge table—the tags from *The Merchant of Venice*; the sharp startling snore, or cry of "That's it!", as one fingered alternative cards in one's hand; such maxims as "There's many a man walking the streets of London with his shirt hanging out of his britches through not drawing trumps."

I cannot remember when I first played contract bridge. Certainly at Wilton Parade, where a fellow "permanent" called Mrs. Laycock, a woman of immense ugliness and charm, was a demon addict. The epoch of playing at Wylie Kay's coincided with Culbertson's great influence on the game. I studied his "Blue Book" with rather more assiduity than the four blue-bound volumes of Stephen's *Commentaries on the Laws of England*, the set book for the Law Society's Intermediate examination. The Wittgensteinian title was apt, for Culbertson's system was intellectually rigorous and in parts odd. The "honour trick" count, the originating and responsive forcing bids, the points evaluation of a purely supporting bid—to mention a few elementary features—would seem stiff to players today, I suppose. But I was already adroit at the play of the cards at a decent family bridge level, and Culbertson showed the way to more scientific things—a way not taken, for I never played the game competitively nor at all in latter times.

A more orthodox form of dissipation for articled clerks also went on: betting on horses. One episode included an elaborate charade about the bookie welshing after a winning week of joint wagering, designed to cause temporary despondency to the third articled clerk, not, I seem to think, permanent loss. Despite his hat by Stetson and his playing in the pack for the Fylde RUFC Second XI, this colleague, nicknamed by Lees rather unjustly but not unconvincingly "Fatty", became something of a butt, though far from the Gorill class. The betting was extremely modest though at one epoch acquired an unpleasant momentum. The uniformed commissionaire, Dalton, an old sweat by definition, had bought or otherwise acquired a betting system called "The 220". From the flat racing calendar 220 races had been chosen, all stakes or plates, no handicaps. The winners of these races were to be backed the next time they ran. If winners again they were dropped from the list. If losers, they were backed once more on their next appearance and then dropped win or lose. At the start of the season in question the system was startlingly successful, the highlight being a 20–1 winner at Yarmouth. Foolishly we increased our stakes. Needless to say, the system fell on evil days, until only Lees and I persevered. At one time

109

no winners at all came up and Lees likened the situation to that of a constipated man. "If we could just expel the hard nut ... " Eventually Lees, too, dropped out, and I was left losing money alone, forced secretly to cash in my only asset, £10 worth of National Savings Certificates—typical of my stubborn support, in several of life's affairs, of dotty logic over common sense. Indeed, I still can't help thinking that with an adequate bank and a staking method (the stake perhaps doubled on a required second bet on any one horse) the system might have been profitable over a number of seasons.

With more resilience Dalton himself acquired a new system, up to a point as rational and plausible as the "220", weights and so forth taken into account. But the final selection depended on the phase of the moon ruling when the race was run, a factor reminiscent of Aunt Maggie's lighting on Spion Kop but by no means so successful. Dalton must be long dead. In the days of my articles we completed property sales and purchases in cash, strange to say; the acceptance in the profession of the banker's draft being in its infancy. Dalton used to be sent to the bank to get the cash required for the day's transactions and on one occasion, as he crossed the windy square near our flat on his way back to the office, some hundreds of pounds in fivers and tenners blew out of his grasp or whatever he was carrying them in. Such was the morality of the times little or no loss was suffered by the firm, people returning the banknotes to Dalton or handing them in to the police. He himself in their position might have been tempted to do otherwise having regard to the depredations of the 220 and moon systems. He
110

bequeathed to me a few words of (presumably) sergeant's Hindi, useful when indicating the direction required in a journey by lift.

Over the long years one inevitably picked up some knowledge of probate work and the simpler conveyancing as well as of bridge and betting. I rather think it was I myself rather than Eric Wylie Kay who felt that this would be a meagre result in the light of the premium paid and time served. Yet as I write this it comes to me that he might have been intent on breaking up that focus of office corruption, the bridge four. At any rate, I moved for a spell down to the litigation section to be instructed in their mysteries. The section was small in relation to the size of the practice as a whole, consisting merely of two men and two rooms on the first floor. There may also have been a girl in the typists' room downstairs. In the section's outer office was a clerk, quite young; tall, thin and pallid, invariably dressed in a dark suit. With his gift for nomenclature Lees called him Docking, and that had supplanted his real surname. J.W. Docking & Son were leading undertakers in the town, familiar in the articled clerks' attic through our entering funeral expenses in a schedule to the affidavits required by the Inland Revenue for estate duty assessment.

One had to go through Docking's office to reach Mr. Ianson's room, overlooking the back street. Harry Ianson was not a partner in the firm though comparatively an elderly solicitor. He had white hair, a red face, big ears, a scattering of fangs, and a voice so loud that on the telephone some claimed he could be clearly heard in the back street. He was a masterly telephoner: initially

111

genial, somewhat vulgar ("the green end of a duck's turd" I once heard him say in a metaphorical context that now escapes me), and liking to employ the machine to try to settle actions or otherwise gain some advantage in them. I think he did not much care to appear in court himself, preferring, if the case could stand it, to brief counsel, usually a stout junior called Edmund Rowson (later a silk) who often visited the office on Saturday mornings to exchange jokes in a voice rivalling Mr. Ianson's in penetration and probably to report on or pick up a brief or two. Occasionally, in actions trivial and by their nature incapable of settlement, Mr. Ianson would have to appear in court himself, and here he used almost exclusively the ingratiating side of his talent, taking up a position on the solicitors' benches close to the box in which his witnesses would appear and then, when addressing the court, working himself by some gradual flanking movement closer to the judge than might seem theoretically possible, all to gain persuasive intimacy.

Though always amiable to me, he lacked the interest (and probably the time) to teach an articled clerk anything much about litigation. Docking, with whom I sat, was like all litigation clerks I have known incapable (or unwilling, the occupation itself encouraging caginess and obduracy) of lucidly and systematically imparting the principles and practice of his job. One of the first things I was put on to was a case where we were acting for an insolvent trader intending to present his own petition in bankruptcy. The steps to be taken remained almost wholly enigmatic, though evidently arranged in Docking's mind in some sort of rational and effective order.

It seemed to me he was not displeased to find me lacking in gumption in such matters, far short of understanding his Kafka world.

In the middle of my articles Mr. Ianson left to become a partner in a firm in a nearby town. Ogden also left: he was given his articles by a solicitor in Blackpool with a view to a partnership when he had qualified, which duly came to pass. Both moves were surprising, prompted somewhat by internal tensions in T. & F. Wylie Kay. For one thing, both moves took place after the death, virtually on the operating table, of Tom Wylie Kay, a shock and grief to all. Despite his tony turn-out he had never really come to terms with "the new Act", as we still called it—the Law of Property Act, 1925, which had come into effect on the 1st January 1926 with the other statutes revolutionizing the law of real property and conveyancing practice. Nor did the internal telephone system, a novelty of the new offices, appeal to him: he preferred to come out of his first-floor room and call or send messages fluttering down to the outer office on the ground floor. He left a good deal of money, even more than came to Auntie Vi, but except for the practice I believe I am right in saying that it was not inherited by Mr. Eric. TWK's death revealed an unsuspected division between uncle and nephew, or perhaps more generally in the family, for the solicitors who acted in the administration of the estate were not T. & F. Wylie Kay but a firm in Manchester.

All this caused a stir in the attic room, not lessened by the additional news that under TWK's will all the clerks were to have suits of mourning. A deep question of interpretation arose. Did the term include articled clerks? The question was resolved in a generous manner, though the rather Victorian bounty was diluted by the decision that the suits were to be made by a client of the firm, a tailor not noted for raglan or ratcatcher or anything to go with a hat by Stetson. "Suits of mourning" was a phrase generally thought to imply black jackets and striped trousers (as worn by me not awfully long before at dancing class and Matins) but Lees, and one or two others infected by his enterprise, ordered a dark lounge suit and so fared better, though I think the jackets were without exception cut without chest seams, like blazers, and hung vilely. With my usual thriftiness I persevered with my outfit until the trousers were impossibly shiny which because of the initial stiffness of the material they fortunately very soon became. I guess Docking was the only one at all pleased with his legacy.*

TWK's death, coupled with the defections of Ogden and Ianson, was the start of a hecatomb at the firm, both metaphorical and actual. Byng left when he qualified, as afterwards did I, and eventually Fatty. The litigation managing clerk who replaced Mr. Ianson committed suicide. I have referred to Lees's going. Eric Wylie Kay

I must add here that, in a letter written in response to his reading this chapter in typescript, Lees says it was I bestowed the name of Docking, the occasion being when the bridge four were waiting in the upper room for TWK's funeral carriages, looking out over the square—across which the litigation clerk was observed hurrying to the office in his new black and stripes, complete with bowler and umbrella. Lees asserts that on seeing this apparition I said: "We shan't be long now—here's Docking."

brought in as a partner his brother-in-law, already in practice in the town, who, however, died quite soon after. Mr. Eric's demise, too, was premature. Driving his car along the promenade, he had a heart attack and ran into the Hotel Metropole at a spot I always imagine to be by the Grill Room entrance, opposite Seacliffe.

By then I had gone from the town. The practice remained a good one, the senior partner a man who like Lees had been given his articles but in my day had been merely the probate managing clerk. As I write this in May 1978 I see in *The Law Society's Gazette* the news of his retirement after sixty-four years with the firm. Had I stayed on after being admitted a solicitor, as Mr. Eric asked me to, how could I have avoided becoming the senior or next senior partner, with strange consequences? How should I have run respectable prosperity along with radical friends and beliefs? What should I have written out of a continuing provincial life?

During the War my wife and son went to Blackpool to escape the London bombing. The Metropole was closed or requisitioned, though a bar under its management, of superior kind, remained open. The entrance to it was near where Higgins & Co. had sold the rock praised by royalty and the jeweller's shop patronised by the Peele girls. In May 1941, on leave from the former boys' shore establishment at Shotley, *HMS Ganges*, where I had done my initial training, my wife and I went into this bar, perhaps on our way to some such entertainment as the nearby Palace Varieties. I was in matelot's garb, bronzed and fit, and embarrassed to be bought a drink by some civilian who made it clear he

115

thought me engaged in active service. What had happened to Frish, I wonder? Perhaps interned with the British fascists and enemy aliens in the Isle of Man—whose outline on some clear evenings one had seen from Wilton Parade against the sunset, bringing thoughts of my brother listening to Amy Woodforde-Finden's piano—safe evenings of only a few years before.

# 6. The Little Railway

In the passage outside the dining-room door at school was a table, normally used only for boarders to pick up their incoming letters. One morning, as we went in to breakfast, instead of letters (or perhaps the letters were overlain) it contained the recumbent form of Ettaboo. He held on his plump stomach (a height convenient for most of the passing boys, though a good few of them, instead of reading the message, committed some physical assault on its bearer) a piece of paper on which was written the voting in the Blackpool constituency in the General Election of the previous day. I think this must have been the election of December 1923, for surely Major Malloy, the Liberal candidate, was shown on Ettaboo's abdomen as victorious over his Tory opponent, and I see from the twenty-sixth edition of *Pears' Cyclopaedia*, itself a relic of those days, in the "Dictionary of Events", that what happened on the third of that month was "Mr. Baldwin's policy defeated, 259 Conservatives elected, 191 Labour, 165 Liberals and others". A Liberal voted in in Blackpool denoted deep radicalism elsewhere.

Possibly on this occasion my emotions were not much engaged, though presumably I was surprised at the Tory candidate's defeat. He may well have been the elegant Sir Walter de Freece, who had married the famous music-hall male impersonator Vesta Tilley. The arrival of the Labour Party into second place in Parliament prefigured my Conservative alderman grandfather's acknowledgement of the chimpanzees' tea-party quality of the breed. During my later years at school I became convinced of the justice and feasibility of socialism and at the General election of 1927 (the local result of which was not, as I recall, announced to the boys by Ettaboo) I proclaimed my allegiance to Labour, a position still highly unrespectable for the provincial middle-classes. I arrived at the belief through reading the polemical side of Wells and Shaw, after being captivated by their imaginative work. One or two experiences in this line of the hero of *The Ruined Boys* incline to the autobiographical so I will not go into details of conversion. Because of the name I was deceived into feeling chuffed at the size of the German National Socialist election vote (could that have been as early as 1924 or as late as 1928?) and though I quickly tumbled to the party's real nature I was not introduced to Marxism-Leninism until I had been left school for two or three years. In any case I was sidetracked from politics by coming across D.H. Law-rence I suppose just about the time I did leave school, and was greatly taken with his adolescent notions of

118

society being changed by men paying more regard to the instinctual side of life. Even his most cock-eyed notions, like the value of wearing tight red trousers (the relevant piece may be found in his journalism and I believe in *Lady Chatterley*), appealed to me—and to Leslie, the pianist friend I had made at school.

I see now when I try to shock by uttering reactionary views as I once achieved a similar effect by leftism, that being part of a minority has always been for me a natural role. Of course, in serious art the position has been inevitable in my time; and in politics I must not discount the hope given by the principles of international socialism even as late as 1931, a hope quite aside from any rather perverse pleasure in feeling oneself the repository of some more or less esoteric or unobvious truth. Why one should always want to ally oneself with the underdog is not altogether clear. One is tempted to discount utterly any virtue in the matter: I mean why should trying to see that a certain one-clawed pigeon gets more than its fair share of bread on the lawn, as has been a concern for some months, reflect creditably on the bread-scatterer? More likely, as a great horror of violence is said to mask a sadistic nature, the conscientious underdog-lover is demonstrating the depth of his self-pity and self-love.

I cannot remember whether Ettaboo was the nickname under which the Headmaster's son was generally known among his schoolfellows or merely a sobriquet invented and used only by my brother and me. It was intended to indicate Kennie's way of talking (he had some impediment, or infantile speech hangover), perhaps his way of pronouncing his own surname. He was nearer my

119

brother's age than mine and so my brother, staying on at the school for a while after I had left, was able to amplify Ettaboo's legendary character and exploits. Poor Ettaboo: neither boarder nor day-boy, his position must have been difficult, though at the time one saw him only as some privileged and therefore detested heir, especially favoured in the matter of diet, as seemed evidenced by his embonpoint. Besides, the imagination boggles at being under the Boss' eye pretty well at all times. Still, I have no doubt he was blessed with proper paternal love. He was often addressed or referred to by the Headmaster as "Master Kenneth", even as "Master Kennie", an extension of the various magisterial uses of name and that title, mainly indicating the respect and formality owed by third parties to a scion of the ruling family—much as a monarch might as a matter of course prefix in conversation his son's name with "Prince", not excluding the affectionate diminutive.

Ettaboo had succeeded to his father's great cranium but the distinguished good looks were lacking, certainly at pre-pubertal age. On top of the cranium Ettaboo wore what seemed a curiously small school-cap, though perhaps it was the largest available. Yet I seem to think that the Boss was not dissatisfied with his son's appearance, even approving of his ample figure, in the manner of Squeers's fond observation of young Wackford: "Here's flesh . . . Why, you couldn't shut a bit of him in a door, when he's had his dinner." I daresay, though, the Boss may have regretted that his son was still unable to follow his constant enjoinder to the school to speak out.

I doubt if I shared such things as the uniqueness of

Ettaboo with Leslie. Our friendship, though not utterly solemn, was sustained by music and books. It was marked from the start with his selflessness. For mid-morning "lunch" he always brought to school bacon sandwiches, his mother's dab hand at cooking revealed even by these, for he fell into the habit of sharing them with me; eventually, after I had met his mother and she had seen that I was "a nice boy", bringing an extra supply especially for me. What a delicacy compared with the school cuisine! Even Ettaboo did not fare so well: well-buttered new white bread, the fat of the bacon crisp, even slightly burnt, for Leslie's mother's culinary style inclined to the successfully reckless and lavish.

Leslie was slender and not tall, long straight nose and smallish chin lending him a starling-like appearance. His intellectual interests and physical slightness did not prevent him from being the school's very effective centre-forward. His adroit style of play, particularly his heading—indeed, his general appearance—was recalled many years later by Charlie Vaughan, a centre-forward who played for Charlton Athletic and far too seldom for representative elevens. As to his being bitten by the Lawrentian bug, I remember after we had left school quite accidentally seeing and being impressed by a line of verse he had written: "If you call, I shall come"—very Look We Have Come Throughish. But he was utterly secretive about his literary work, and I do not recall showing him mine, though very likely I did. We were ardent pursuers of what we thought vital in culture, the opportunities for exercising such a role in the provinces of the late twenties being restricted beyond today's conception. On one occasion we realised neither of us had ever heard Beethoven's Fifth Symphony. The enormity of the omission made me with Vi-like extravagance then and there ask my mother to fund the purchase of the records. We went straight to the shop and bought the album of four black label HMV records conducted by Sir Landon Ronald, the cost twenty-four shillings, a tidy sum. The discs were already elderly but I hadn't yet become fastidious about recordings. A lot of music then had a shock effect. I remember playing the first movement of Mozart's late G minor symphony, recently acquired, one summer afternoon by the open window of the flat overlooking the Metropole, the opening subject, except for its final cadence, sounding to me staggeringly modern. I expect I was also conscious that a few of the holiday-makers perambulating below, including some beautiful and intelligent girl, might well hear the strains and think that in the unusually chic and convenient premises high above dwelt an appropriately lofty intelligence. Insane intellectual and amatory fantasies of adolescence, unspeakable yearnings and frustrations of that epoch, so prolonged, seemingly unassuagable! I would not like to have to write about them again, as either reality or fiction, let alone relive them.

Leslie's uncle by marriage was a radio buff, his apparatus complicated, unreliable, low fidelity, bits of it actually being changed during reception—bits that when I became a compulsory buff during the War I realised had been inductances. We went to his house to hear a broadcast of Bartok quartets (or, more likely, a concert which included one of them). The music, dimly heard through shared earphones, was a revelation. "Another Beethoven" I pronounced. One year, almost certainly 1929, we holidayed together in London with our respective mothers and my brother. On arrival, after a testing journey by charabanc, Leslie and I beat it to the Queen's Hall to a Promenade Concert, standing stoically in the "promenade". Sir Henry Wood usually left the last item in the second half to be conducted by the orchestra's leader, Charles Woodhouse. By then the promenade had become less congested and one might be lucky enough to see Sir Henry look in for a minute or two—perhaps curious about the orchestra's sound or Woodhouse's ability—wearing a soft black hat, on his way home to that domesticity later revealed to be so unhappy for him.

Needless to say, the leader of the Queen's Hall Orchestra did not conduct with his bow, violin in the other hand, as was the practice of Mons. Spiro, a noted Blackpool musical figure—indeed, an exponent of that pier-end music from which Leslie helped to wean me. Mons. Spiro was always billed thus, never M. Spiro; and if his Christian name was ever disclosed, which is doubtful, I have forgotten it, as in the case of Hamlet. Balding, short, with full lips and pince-nez, Mons. Spiro looked like a plumper Stravinsky. The latter would probably not have approved of the Spiro style—joining in the tuttis only at climaxes, frequently inserting a gratuitous solo violin part, and playing during the interval in the ray of a spotlight. The intervals in question were at the Palace Cinema, in the same building as the Palace Varieties where Joe Jackson had failed to make the Boss laugh. Mons. Spiro's orchestra was easily big enough to have

123

included Archie Gladman's double-bass. It was eventually displaced at the Palace by the talkies but I seem to think Mons. Spiro returned to or took up an appointment on the North Pier.

I cannot remember if Leslie and I glimpsed Sir Henry on that first night. When we returned to the Regent Palace Hotel my mother told me that she and Leslie's mother, with my brother, had strolled out after dinner to find a likely cinema, which they did in the Haymarket. The ladies had been baffled by the film on show, though my brother's laughter had dislodged him from his seat. But even he found difficulty in describing what he had seen. Despite the pleasures of the concert I felt jealous, for after a brief spell of resistance to the shocking American voices and general vulgarity I had succumbed to the talkies as I had to silent pictures. The film had been *The Cocoanuts*.

The fresh cast of characters my life recruited after I left school was partly formed from the shops and business establishments by which the new flat was surrounded. Among these personages was Mr. Meng or, rather, M. Meng, for despite his oriental name he was French, though not proclaiming the fact as ostentatiously as Mons. Spiro. He had a ladies hairdressing salon and was said to be not at all frustrated in his romantic ambitions. His son, also M. Meng (for such was his initial), did look more Chinese (of the giant kind exhibited in Victorian times like Chang, "the tall man of Fychow"), and had been at school with me and my brother, who was delighted with the characters, appearance, name, and possibility of observation of both father and son. The

124

owner of a furniture shop and his wife became friendly with my mother, who in fact in much later days went to live with the wife, by then widowed, as a paying guest, and through that met my step-father. Moreover, my brother was at one time engaged to the attractive daughter; but of course this again lay pretty far into a future to be strangely unfolded. Below our flat was a flat and workroom belonging to Madame Pym and below that, on the promenade, the milliner's shop she owned. Madame Pym was not a compatriot of Mons. Spiro, despite her title—that being assumed to better her trade image. At one period she had staying with her and working in the shop an extremely good-looking niece with whom I had a brief, innocent, unsatisfactory affair, conducted mainly in an unsatisfactory place, namely the access staircase referred to previously which petered out so curiously between the two parts of our flat. There had been a boy at school appropriately called P. King, for like Meng *fils* his aspect was somewhat Chinese. At the flat his aunt, if aunt she was, came into our lives, I think initially because she was in the nursing profession and she gave therapy of some sort to my mother. I was dashed when she expressed herself weary of *The Ring* because of my repeated playing of a couple of records of the start of *Rhinegold*. She was not young but on the other hand by no means too old for exchanges of an unofficial kind, a point I may well have taken on board. But my desires were for unattainable nieces rather than skittish aunts.

About this time my appearance changed considerably. I grew my hair longer and gave up my devotion to Pears' Solidified Brilliantine (though to be strictly accurate, fashion in the anointing of hair had changed shortly before I left school, a fluid called "Anzora"—or its greasy sister, "Anzora Viola"—coming into favour. It kept the hair in place, even retaining the corrugations of the comb, but lent it the feel of cardboard, as though one were wearing some helmet designed for children to "dress up" in. No doubt it was this I gave up.) My hair, previously straight, became wavy. It was still the day of shirts with separate collars but I liked as far as possible to wear my old cricket shirts (plus tie) so as to get a desirable low-cut Byronic effect, a style I fear Mr. Southworth would have thought the reverse of nutty. These arrangements clashed with the sartorial image I had evolved for myself immediately I had left school, and for some time I went hatless, eschewing the pre-Slasher Green overcoat, favouring instead a mackintosh cut rather long that had been made for me from traditional biscuit-hued material supplied by Mr. Fraser from the rubber-proofing mill.

This was a time, too, when I got to know the heart of Manchester, previously only a fragmentary memory from childhood. A recent requirement had made it necessary for a solicitor's articled clerk to attend a year's law school. The nearest place where the statutory lectures were held was Manchester University. On Mondays and Thursdays in term time I travelled to Manchester for the day. On one of the days I got up very early to go to some lectures on contract and tort, part of the ordinary law degree course, which articled clerks were entitled but not obliged to attend. In winter I rose in the dark and walked through the dark along the promenade to the station, the moon perhaps over the sea, the dawn just breaking in
126

the opposite sky, only one or two other pedestrians challenged in the waning dusk. The wind would blow the shutters, if any, of the Metropole (quitted as I started off) and my abundant, ungreasy, unanzoraed locks, and twine the skirts of my mackintosh about my shins. In my stomach (prematurely, the stomach sensed) were two boiled eggs. I persuaded my mother that she at least need not appear at such an ungodly hour, so I had the alarm clock. That I should make my own breakfast was not at all part of my mother's conception of the feminine role, and that I should start the day other than by eating bacon and egg seemed to her gravely disadvantageous (though she did not concede that I was capable of or would have time for preparing that dish). She even put the water in the egg pan the night before.

I would sway through the yellow winter gloom on the upper deck of the rather well-designed Manchester trams, probably sitting in the ship-like enclosed stern or prow, over-concerned at getting out down Oxford Road at the right stop for the University. I cannot exaggerate my seriousness about the trivialities of life, lack of know-how, nervousness, shyness—coupled, though of course it is hard to judge how effectively, with masks designed to hide my deficiencies. As to the right tram-stop syndrome, a recurring anxiety dream to this day concerns the last hour in a foreign hotel; the bill not paid, traveller's cheques not cashed, next destination unfixed but a vital train time imminent, the room where the luggage is still not packed unable to be found. As to masks assumed, these may often have been mistaken for conscious superiority of one kind or another, so I judge in the light of

127

impressions conveyed to others which have leaked to me in later life. A strange penalty for shyness is to be completely misunderstood.

Most of the time until the afternoon lectures, the compulsory part for articled clerks, I would spend going round the bookshops. Through parsimony (really, as in my mother's case, to preserve the family fortune not my own pocket) I missed a good many desirable acquisitions, though I was never a serious collector nor willing to risk more than a few bob. On the other hand, as with the 220 System, I occasionally foolishly plunged. In this category I would put a first edition of David Garnett's *The Sailor's Return*, the author then widely accounted an exceptional young novelist; even the first American edition of *The Captain's Doll*, though that might now recoup the six shillings expended, if only through inflation. The winter in question would be that of 1929–30, for I see that my copy of *Dubliners*, which I certainly bought on one of those spendthrift occasions for two shillings, is inscribed "March 1930" under my signature on the flyleaf. The edition is the second edition published by the Egoist Press in 1922, which opposite the title page announced: "In Preparation *Ulysses*". (At the time I am writing about the latter work was banned and remained so for a number of years, more tantalizing for those, like me, who wanted to copy its fictional techniques than possible corruptees. When I met John Davenport, I rather think in the summer following this very winter, he told me of two or three Charing Cross Road booksellers who might well supply me with the illegal article on mentioning his name. But when this ploy was tried, doubtless with guilt and trepidation, it did not work, and one had to be content with extracts from the novel that appeared in critical works and the memory of Gorill's story in similar style). It was in 1930 that in the train back from Manchester (with typical thriftiness overlooking some-one's evening paper) I read of D.H. Lawrence's death, shocking as the death of Byron in a former day, and probably helping me and others to turn from follies concerning the personal life to political involvement, more appropriate to the age but also not lacking in wacky illusions.

Thursday nights were Hallé concerts nights, for which I often stayed, stayed, journeying back to Blackpool by the last train. The seats I favoured in the old Free Trade Hall were under the side balcony, cheap but near. What arrived as novelties in those days must be marvelled at again: I need only instance a first hearing of *Eine Kleine Nachtsmusik*, which left one with a sense of a common-place genre transcended with amazing resourcefulness, and a set of marvellous melodies just beyond recall. The permanent conductor was Hamilton Harty, florid of face, not much in my line then with his practical advocacy of Berlioz and his own typically British compositions—do I dream that I actually heard his tone poem "With the Wild Geese" and the scherzo from his "Irish" symphony? But now I see more clearly than in those days of yore that he was not unenterprising as a programme builder and also did quite a bit for modern music. When the fine records of Constant Lambert's *The Rio Grande* came out, the Hallé was conducted by the composer and,

129

astonishing me, the piano part brilliantly played by Harty.

It was in the year I first went to boarding school that the curious entertainment *Façade* was offered to a London audience. Behind a curtain in the Aeolian Hall were six instrumentalists, the composer W.T. Walton and the poet Edith Sitwell. A feature of the painted curtain was a head with an open mouth, the latter being the outlet of a patent megaphone through which the poet read some of her poems while the instrumentalists played musical numbers under the composer's direction. Osbert Sitwell was MC; Sacheverell Sitwell had discovered the megaphone. The Sitwell siblings were, of course, notorious members of the post-war avant garde: their work influenced me quite a bit when I started seriously to write verse. Their friend Walton was a young man from Oldham whose music when *Façade* was first performed had never been before the public. He later revised and expanded the numbers from *Façade* and the work was enterprisingly recorded by Decca, the poet joined as reader by Constant Lambert. Leslie bought these records and I can still attempt an impression of Edith Sitwell's rendering: in timbre and enunciation the voice greatly resembled that of Nellie Wallace, a music-hall comic of a just-past day (of whom, indeed, Edith Sitwell was an admirer). A further connection with the halls comes to mind. After the War I met the poet two or three times at John Lehmann's parties. By then she was of such an eminence that selected guests were one by one invited to sit by her. As I once waited in the wings, as it were, William Plomer whispered to me: "Isn't she exactly like

Max Miller?" There was certainly some resemblance in the long nose and smooth skin, but the association was really made plausible by the poet's wearing a species of white bowler hat (though Max Miller would surely not have added the plume).

I myself bought the Decca recording of Walton's overture *Portsmouth Point*. It is a congested piece and sounded even more so on a ten-inch 78 of the epoch. It was no more to my mother's taste than *Rhinegold* to Miss King's. Moreover, she off-handedly claimed a familiar acquaintance with the composer: as a girl or young woman she had taken singing lessons from Mr. Walton and had often passed his son Willie playing on the pavement outside the house. This amazing revelation probably came after I had seen the young composer conduct the Hallé in the orchestral suite he had made out of *Façade*. He was tall, pallid, awkward, and when conducting carried his left arm as though in a sling, plainly obeying the precept that in the conductor's art the batonless arm has no proper function. I may add that my mother's brother John told me in a letter in the last years of his life that his music master at Hulme Grammar School had been William Walton's brother Noel, especially remembered for his enthusiasm for the part-song "Nymphs and Shepherds, Come Away."

The Hallé also performed on Mondays in a series of a more popular kind called the "Municipal" concerts. I stayed for one of these, then found to my extreme horror, at the station, that the late train to Blackpool did not run on Mondays. I was marooned. I managed to get a message by telephone to my mother, then set off to stay the night

131

in Oldham with my grandparents. This solution seemed resourceful (the notion of a hotel in Manchester was presumably rejected through lack of cash or, conceivably, thriftiness) but I could not give forewarning. I changed terminuses in Manchester and took the Oldham train.

There was no real reason why the order and nomenclature of the stations between Manchester and Oldham should be greatly familiar or have Proustian undertones, for in my father's day the journey would be made by motor-car and later our visits to Oldham from Blackpool were not awfully frequent, and indeed were latterly made again by car, my mother going in for one in the very early thirties. Yet the names had a significance for me such as the poet W. J. Turner found in Chimborazo and Cotopaxi; and of course the places themselves had some associations and physical features that memory retained. I have not looked them up. The line may even have been lopped by the Beeching axe. I will guess that the stations were Miles Platting, Newton Heath, Failsworth, Hollinwood, Werneth, Mumps.

Newton Heath must not be taken to indicate any countryside, however exiguous, between Manchester and Oldham: the urban brick was unbroken. Failsworth being the place of my parents' first house was also the home of childhood friends, most forgotten, a few recalled. How did we come to know the Richardsons? He was an actor or, more accurately, music-hall performer, perhaps best known in pantomime where he had been the King figure to Little Tich's Dame. My mother cared for the art neither of Little Tich nor of Arnold Richardson but since she must surely have been wrong about Little Tich

132

she may also have erred in the other case. However, I remember a postcard, printed for propaganda purposes like the photograph of Uncle John as "Violet", depicting Mr. Richardson as a square-faced man of middle-age wearing a crown, seemingly of no great individuality or humour. Like many husbands of the era he died prematurely so I never myself saw him perform. We continued to be friendly with the widow and her child of my own age, the former famous for plucking whiskers from her chin behind a guarding hand, tweezers hidden in the other, chatting nonchalantly, a slight jerk of the head, like a nervous tic, indicating occasional success.

In Failsworth, too, lived the Peeles, our closest friends when my father was alive and to whose house, somewhat impressively set back in the main Manchester to Oldham Road, I was sent—I have said following my father's death until after his funeral but I wonder if this was so and whether the time might not have been that of the birth and early death of my youngest sibling Eric, which occurred during my father's terminal illness. Certainly I have no memories of Eric's brief life, though I am almost certain his death occurred in hospital. The doubt here is perhaps characteristic of the misunderstandings of childhood but surely has been augmented by self-centred obtuseness. Mr. Peele was a well-to-do mill manager, dark, quiet, good-looking. His wife was an incongruous mate, it now seems: plump, jolly and, as it turned out, a secret drinker. Their two daughters were older than me, the younger by not so much. They were allowed—seemed, to my envy, to have the right—to go every Tuesday to the cinema almost opposite their house, thus keeping up with the serials which in those days came on before the "big picture", a stroke of lifemanship marvellous to me. They were taken by the maid, Annie Fleury, who came from the Channel Islands and whose younger sister Emily had come to work for us.

Those sisters from Guernsey: Annie's face I am able to summon up, but though I know that Emily was fairer, better-looking, her image has almost wholly faded. In an "autograph album" which had been given me by my grandparents at the Christmas of 1917, Emily wrote the following, signing it and adding the date "April 1920"—the month of my father's will, the year of his death:

> Never trouble trouble till trouble troubles you.
> It's an old and musty saying
> But it's very often true
> If you never trouble trouble
> It will never trouble you.

The lines were memorable from the start and even the hand that set them down may still be alive, for another maid of the same epoch, Nellie Straw—splendid name—wrote to me out of the blue only a few years ago when for some reason my name had been in the newspapers. But even Hardy might have been gravelled to wring meaning or the lack of it from such residuary orts.

The Peeles, like us when my father was alive, used to take a furnished house for a month in the summer. One year (probably more than one) they rented Mrs. Vero's house: hence my mother taking rooms there at a later

134

and sadder date. We rented the next-door house. The Veros would not be in a residence, of course, so I do not know whether in those days the grave chords of "Willie Vero" were yet to be heard. I played with the Peele girls in the back gardens of the adjoining houses, sometimes making "brooches" out of leaves, flowers and berries in competition for the most beautiful. They had ample pocket money: once I went with them to the jeweller's near Higgins & Co. in the row of Metropole shops where the older girl bought a little gilt egg which could be opened to reveal tiny opal eggs in a nest of cotton wool. The aesthetic sense shown impressed me, though I was worried by the inutility of the object. Plainly the elder girl must have been the instigator of the brooches game. She was like her father in disposition and looks. Mr. Peele inscribed a bible "with fondest love" from himself and his wife to my father, dating it "Christmas 1920". Whether my father derived any comfort from it or even saw it must be doubtful, because he died exactly a week before Christmas Day. The inscription is in Mr. Peele's somewhat conventional but extremely graceful hand, carefully done, probably on pencilled guide lines, subsequently erased. The compassion involved may be imagined.

Mrs. Peele was the sort of person who might well have introduced us to the Richardsons and also to Mrs. Gee, a friend of very early days who gave my brother and me napkin rings at our christenings, still in daily use. Mine, even in 1912, was William Morrisy in its engraved decoration. My brother's, four years later, was quite "modern" in its plainness: just one more example of my luck in life, as I used to think. I only dimly recall Mrs. Gee—imperious, enormous, seated in a drawing-room full of knick-knacks like a sinister character in a story by Walter de la Mare. It was said she ate half a dozen eggs for breakfast; other dietetic details, now forgotten, were equally sensational. It comes to me that she lived at Newton Heath, which may have had its salubrious parts after all.

Hollinwood was, of course, the place of the rubber-proofing mill; also the nearest station to my grandparents' house in Hollins Road. Perhaps it was that dark Monday night, peering anxiously out from the carriage window, that the successive station names were finally imprinted. How did I find my way so late from the station to the bottom of Hollins Road to catch the appropriate tram? The route was not straightforward and I doubt whether I had ever taken it alone before. Even at seventeen or eighteen I would be apprehensive about missing the way, asking directions.

When I got off the tram I would have a short walk up the quite steep road to the house, passing Frederick Street, where my brother had been born and my father had read newspapers full of the First War. The house was in darkness when I rang the bell. My grandmother appeared in night attire, eventually reassured to find my presence portending no more than a missed train. I do not recall my grandfather being on the scene. Perhaps he was still playing bridge at the Conservative Club. Indeed, virtually nothing remains in my memory of the occasion beyond a sense (which I may be retrospectively importing), through that late encounter, of my grandmother's eventual widowhood which was prolonged into the period of the Second War; amazingly and inappropriately, as it seems to me now, experiencing some of those awful days. My grandfather retired in 1933, died, I think, in 1937. Who knows whether what he achieved, as mayor, alderman, justice of the peace, and so forth, enabling my grandmother to play her largely supporting role with dignity and humour, compensated her for characteristics of his she may have found too eccentric or insensitive, to say nothing of the inevitable stifling of her own talents? Certainly he left her in reduced circumstances, as they say. Among my mother's few surviving papers was a notebook in my grandmother's writing recording the periodical sums (usually thirty shillings a week) received from my mother for living expenses (recouped after my grandmother's death from the proceeds of sale of the Hollins Road house, which I imagine to have been my grandparents' only asset of any substance).

In my grandfather's presence, in his latter days, I expect I kept dark my socialist beliefs and literary tastes. In my penultimate year at school, on a visit to Blackpool, he had taken me to buy a pair of spiked running shoes, which probably were decisive in my victory in the 100 and 220 yards in the first of my two successive victorious years, to say nothing of breaking the school long jump record with 19 ft. 5½ ins. in my last year. His trouble and generosity were not characteristic but pride in heredity was tapped: he had once been amateur sprint champion of Lancashire. His finding a shop that stocked the things and his knowledge of the type and fit required

137

impressed me a lot. His concern with the practicalities of life was usually strictly limited: the buying of prize cheese, for instance, or washing the small change he had been given in shops or on the tram. He may have been disappointed that I had dropped athletics—all sport—after leaving school. As to literature, he had once picked up a slim volume of W.H. Davies brought into the house by me, read it in about twenty minutes, and remarked: "Not much in that." That would have been in my *John o' London*'s epoch, when Georgians were still OK, but the galling thing was I felt his judgement fundamentally justified. On the other hand, Lawrence would have had little more appeal.

That night I expect I slept in the room that in my childhood I had known as Uncle Freddy's. Being at the front of the house it was well situated to hear the trams as they rattled down Copster Hill Road and ground round the sharp corner into Hollins Road as though about to run into the house itself, which was fairly high above the road but separated from it by only a small front garden. The view was of the modest park where as a boy I had played bowls on the two crown greens and talked to Ernest, the park-keeper, who my mother maintained, with only faint exaggeration, had teeth to match the colour of his bowling arenas. There was no back garden, just a tiny concreted yard, bounded by coal-place, WC, and wash-house, places of some interest on boyhood visits—even the WC, dark in spite of its white-washed walls. It had a scrubbed unpainted seat and was equipped not with a roll but squares of newspaper hanging by a string from a hook, good enough for my grandparents' servant (who I suppose was the principal user) faithful and loved though she was. In the wash-house was a mangle with a wheel and cogs of high capitalistic substantiality, the wooden rollers fraying slightly in the middle with decades of use. On the shelves were a few substances appealing to the instincts later so developed by the Boss that I matriculated in Inorganic Chemistry with a high mark—among them linseed oil and whiting which I had read somewhere (perhaps in a bound volume of *The Scout*) were the ingredients of putty, as I pleasurably proved.

Messing about in the back-yard (also in the lane running along the side of the house where, opposite, a chicken-run was fenced by planks containing, for a reason never discovered, an occasional tiny ceramic cylinder which could be prised out and acquired) one was in touch with the kitchen, equipped with a coal-fired "range" as solid as the mangle and in which bread was made, the process ending with muffins (thin, holey, the outside faintly leathery) evolved on a baking-stone on the cooling oven floor. I was impressed by my mother some-times efficiently taking the lead in this, though at Water-head insulated from such chores by Emily Fleury, Nellie Straw and the like, vigorously kneading the dough which when risen might be compared by some family vulgarian to a pale, fat, nude bottom.

On the surprise visit in question I wonder if I looked in the commodious airing cupboard in the bathroom to see if bars of soap were still kept on the slats and on the floor the set of illustrated books about the history of Britain, maybe of the whole Empire, looked at in earlier

139

days. The Empire would be a concept already distasteful, yet when I had first gone to boarding school not many years before I was proud of the extent of red on a Mercator's map of the world depicted by one of my Canadian stamps, which bore the legend "WE HOLD A VASTER EMPIRE THAN HAS BEEN". I expect I examined my pimples in my grandfather's magnifying shaving-mirror on the window-still. The next morning I went back to Manchester on the little railway and must have been absurdly late for the office, ruining the bridge four. As I add this superfluous facetiousness some faint idea is borne in on me of my grandmother saying goodbye to her eldest grandchild above the tramlines, before the vista of the park, and not entirely hiding emotion. On the other hand, one must not underestimate Oldhamers' stiff and silent lip on pretty well all life's occasions, facetiousness being, in fact, part of that process.

I do not believe I ever alighted at Werneth Station. Just before the War I wrote with Julian Symons a never-performed play, a political satire set in an imaginary Europe, a genre sufficiently indicated by the prose parts of the Auden-Isherwood *On the Frontier*. Two characters I christened Mr. Failsworth and General Werneth, right-wing union leader and politico respectively, the names seeming of sufficient ambiguity for a non-specific nationality—"Failsworth" typing the character in ancient dramatic tradition; "Werneth" possibly being imagined to have the pronunciation "Vairnet". (After writing this I found in *A Centenary History of Oldham* by Hartley Bateson that the old form of Werneth was Vernet). I went to my first school in Werneth, not far short of a mile walk from the Frederick Street house. Beyond a dim vision of a flight of steps up to the school door, my only memory of my brief attendance is an instance of early odiousness. A member of a group who walked to school my way became top of the class, a place I coveted. After school I encouraged the rest of the group to run off and leave him in the lurch, calling out with vile antagonism: "We never had anything to do with the last top-of-the class." Such a phrase sounds stilted and sophisticated for a six-year-old but I do not doubt it is close to the *ipsissima verbae*. I was secretly and immediately ashamed of them once uttered, for no age is too young to be aware of ill conduct.

Even a denizen of Oldham must be conscious of the strange nomenclature of the locality Mumps. A lowish railway bridge across the main road; perhaps greater damp and dark than elsewhere; a nadir reached—such features reinforced the connotations of depression and disease. When we moved from Frederick Street to Waterhead I had to go to Mumps to attend a dame's school, though by tram not rail, Waterhead being on Mumps's farther side. I used to call for a neighbour's child, Marjorie Marsland, on the way to the tram. On leaving the house she made her long black stockings simulacra of a boy's "golf" stockings by pulling her thin elastic garters below her knees and turning the stockings down. She may also have got rid of other trappings of femininity: certainly she used to slip the constraining elastic of her hat from under her chin and tuck it into the crown. All this evidence of a strong character and a wish to be liberated (an additional and more fundamental aspect of

141

which is given in *The Perfect Fool*) did not make her any the less attractive as a companion. Though I recall an occasion in our nursery when my bare leg rested against hers (perhaps she always turned her stockings down away from home), I do not think feelings went much beyond friendship. She was already a pupil at the school and like Vergil guided me through the initial purgatories of its routines and the journey to them.

A week or two before I wrote the foregoing paragraph, Marjorie Yates, the widow of the Metropole pianist who had helped to oblige the Prussian with Smetana's overture, came for lunch bringing a book of reproductions of paintings by the Lancashire primitive, Helen Bradley. It had been bought by Marjorie's daughter, brought up in Blackpool but married to an American lawyer, and stunned to see in a Washington bookshop a dust-jacket of a Blackpool railway station, albeit depicting it as it was in 1908. She had sent the book to her mother. I opened it at random. The page showed Buckley & Proctor's drapers shop at Mumps in the same epoch. Near the shop an arrow on a public lavatory wall indicated the direction of Mumps Station. I doubt if I had seen or heard "Buckley & Proctor" for almost sixty years, yet the names were as familiar as Debenham & Freebody. The other Marjorie and I had passed the shop every time we got off the tram from Waterhead.

Some forgotten actress or other heroine of the masses may have made popular the name Marjorie for girls who grew up with me. Even the niece of the bogus "little French milliner" was called Marjorie. I felt a lack of consistency when the girl I was to marry proved to be

142

called Kathleen but reassurance came when she told me that her parents nearly had her christened Marjorie. "Joan" ran Marjorie close. Skeltonic and Shakespearean names: even now when their possessors are in their mid-sixties—Joan Eastwood perhaps seventy!—they trail romance.

One publication I did buy in Manchester without miserly qualms during my law school year was Lawrence's *Nettles*, published in Faber & Faber's "Criterion Miscellany" at a shilling. I took it to the afternoon lectures in the statutory series and had it in front of me on the desk, no doubt from the same motive that had prompted me to play Mozart near an open window. The lecturer picked up the bright red pamphlet with a grin. Lawrence's name was generally known, I expect through the recent publication of *Lady Chatterley's Lover*, though perhaps it had had significance ever since the banning of *The Rainbow*. I seem to think the lecturer was a bright fellow who went to the Bar and was eventually elevated to the Bench: he read out a few lines at random and genially asked me if I thought it was poetry. The idea of Lawrence being vulnerable in that way seemed to me very *vieux chapeau*. The poem may have been one called "The British Workman and the Government":

> Hold my hand, Auntie, Auntie,
> Auntie hold my hand!
> I feel I'm going to be naughty, Auntie
> and you don't seem to understand.

The poem later contains a passage reminiscent of

143

Stephen Spender's "Now You've No Work, Like a Rich Man", which was in the *Oxford Poetry* of the year of *Nettles* and I think had earlier appeared in the *Criterion*. Though one did not quite realise it yet, for the young writer the world of David Garnett and the Sitwells and Major Malloy and Sir Walter de Freece had ceased to have significance.

*A Portrait of the Artist*, the cheap edition of *Point Counterpoint*, both bought in the year I bought *Dubliners*; and imitations of the techniques of *Ulysses*—such as these brought a new aim to my writing of fiction, on the whole disastrous. Certainly not until round about the start of the War was I able actually to finish a novel and that has rightly stayed unpublished. The worst aspects of experimentalism usually attract the bad or novice writer, and I was no exception. I recall seriously outlining to Leslie the scheme of a projected fiction: it would begin quite normally (and by that, in those days, I would mean fixedly inside the protagonist's head, *à la* Dalloway) and gradually get more and more boring, ending with long Latin quotations. Presumably this was to depict some adolescent or provincial agony. Any consideration for the reader's enlightenment let alone pleasure, or any ingratiatory quality in the author, was not allowed for, such was the pervasiveness of "modernism", still not exhausted today and by no means emanating solely from survivors of the epoch like Samuel Beckett.

The new or, rather, renewed impulse to write prose fiction seemed particularly associated with my bi-weekly journeys to Manchester, even with the fresh glimpse of the little railway. The navy-blue, black-sleeved waistcoats worn by porters in those days; the pungency of station urinals; the noise and bitter smell of steam exuded like some sudden excretory relief from under locomotives; the compartments' dusty upholstery, of idiosyncratic texture and pattern; dawn breaking or dusk falling beyond shaded yellow station lights; above all, the chance of amatory adventure among fellow travellers and at the end of journeys—I expect such things could be found in all my botched fiction of the time. As would what Peter Quennell in his volume of autobiography, *The Marble Foot*, has well described as the "single terrifying or disgusting image"—images from reality I collected as I collected the titles of those rare novels (*The Old Wives' Tale*, for instance, and *A Passage to India*) which I considered gave a true sensation of the detailed length yet swift passage of life, and the meaning of its lack of meaning. Both images and titles have now been largely dispersed in my mind. As to the former, an example would be of an anthropoid masturbating in its cage at a zoo, eating the semen; but the collection was by no means exclusively sexual.

Such fiction was far from the rational and comprehensive novel envisaged some years after the War, anatomizing small town society, which would have delineated elements that in what for me were my student days (when in a quite real sense everyday life seemed poetic life) I took little artistic account of: for instance, the smart social events of the year, the Spinsters' and Benedicts' Balls, Mr. Eric himself being on the organizing committee of the latter; the remnants of the families of fishing village days, enriched by the rise in land values or involvement in the entertainment business, major share-holders in the companies running such things as the Palace; the seasonal workers in winter, as idle as articled clerks but rather more impoverished; and the tribe of various landladies, the Barracloughs, Veros and Sideys. Strange that modern English fiction (and films, come to that) has never quite contrived to give its provincial settings the universality and sophistication captured by transatlantic counterparts. No sense of depression, how-ever slight, comes over one when one realises that an American novel or movie is set in a provincial city or even small town. My own novel of provincial life would set out to do at least that. But it never got written: for one reason I found I came to shirk the labour of writing novels which scarcely earned their modest advances and failed to go into paperback or appear in the United States—strange admission, for even through middle-age I did not imagine I was affected in the enterprise of writing by lack of critical or commercial success.

But I must add, apropos of the foregoing, that I suppose for me everyday life has never ceased to seem poetic life, except, of course, for those recurring periods when all poets lose their power of observing, comparing, and writing rhythmically. It could be said that the poetic sense has been too easily satisfied by the life I slipped into; but then, thinking back on the poetry produced, a good part of it is of, say, Baudelairean strangeness. Much could be quoted from Wallace Stevens's letters on this baffling subject of the artist leading a "rather routine life" (as he once phrased it), for example: "While one

146

is never sure that it makes much difference, one is equally never sure that it doesn't."

# 7. Beauty

Like those of war service, memories from childhood incline to be unrepresentatively funny. My brother once wrote home that he had been caned by the Boss for carrying sage. That my mother, though puzzled, did nothing about this harshness over a practice as apparently unvenal as warding off vampires with garlic is not only evidence of her trust in the school but also of her profound acceptance of the *status quo*. It should be said that the orthography of the letter may have been faulty. Sage was a boy, even smaller than Thompson, quite in the Little Tich class, and for ever being lifted by other boys as though he were an engaging doll, so much so that the Boss had issued an edict against the practice. Hilarity ensued when my mother's misunderstanding was subsequently removed but my brother would scarcely have found the episode amusing.

In spite of my schoolboy socialism, later evolving into

something more extreme, I inherited my mother's resignation. It never crossed my mind that with sufficient will I could have opted out of the law—abandoned the daily journeys across the square to the offices of T. & F. Wylie Kay; the prescribed books for the Law Society's Intermediate examination, the four volume of Stephen's *Commentaries on the Laws of England*, plus works on trust accounts and book-keeping; and the positively uncongenial side of a solicitor's practice represented by Docking's world. I went on accepting what I had chosen in ignorance at sixteen. About my mother's affairs I was also peculiarly passive (dread combination of diffidence and narcissism), not least her health. I worried about it, yet helped her not at all, even convinced sometimes that "nerves" and "palpitations" were merely hypochondriacal, little thinking I should myself be a victim of their reality in later years. Her hyperthyroidism remained undiagnosed, and worsened, and the flat on the promenade became too great a burden for her. Once more we moved into "rooms". Whether if I had done more myself in the domestic line or insisted on help from the outside the move could have been avoided I do not know. In any case, perhaps it is looking back from my sessile sixties that makes the change seem more regrettable. My mother's restlessness was not always altogether forced by events and possibly met some inner need.

The rooms were in Blackpool's South Shore, far from T. & F. Wylie Kay's office, past my old school, well on the way, in fact, to the school's playing fields, scene of my athletics triumphs and partnering Gorill at full back. The accomodation may have been found or recommended by Leslie's mother, who then lived nearby. I accepted the inconvenient tram journey to the office, actually coming home for lunch, and the return of Barracloughian conditions. The house or rather "semi-bungalow" was owned by Mrs. Sidey, presumably a widow. She had a son, Victor, and a Pekinese bitch called Beauty. We added our African grey parrot to the household, the only pet we ever had, brought from the Gold Coast (as it then was) by Leslie's father who was a railway official there. I say "pet" but the bird was of uncertain temper. Even with me, who was the most emotionally involved (as in the case of all actually or metaphorically incarcerated), its moods were variable, sometimes when on my shoulder taking an ear-lobe in its beak and increasing the pressure until one was convinced that injury was about to be done. But this was only some Gold Coast tribal test, as it were, and if one stood firm the grip was relaxed in due course. The same rule applied when one scratched its head through the bars of the cage: the bird had to be allowed to snatch at the intruding finger, attempted withdrawal likely to be disastrous.

Beauty had no great appeal, her bad temper more consistent than Polly's and shown in both looks and behaviour, though like many female characters it may be that her worst features stick in the memory. She was certainly a good house dog, the mere utterance of the words "Send them off, Beauty" causing her to rush to the nearest window in a cascade of yapping, though the lurking miscreants had no more reality than Aunt Maggie's detectives. My brother and I sometimes tested her prowess by introducing the triggering words into conversations about quite other matters and with no change of tone: she was rarely, if ever, caught out. Did I count among my stock of "single terrifying or disgusting" images that of finding late at night in the bathroom (where oddly enough she slept), Beauty assuming with her sleeping cushion what was then generally regarded as the male sexual role, having myself returned from similar preoccupations on a level conceived to be altogether more elevated? It could be so, for one's notions generally were extravagantly romantic, so much so that though I have usually hoarded such things I quite soon destroyed a journal-notebook of the period as seen even then to be too embarrassing, in some entries Leslie and I figuring under names I imagined to be more apt than our real ones.

Mrs. Sidey's son Victor was in age between my brother and myself—long-nosed, sallow, old-fashioned. He was as taken with the parrot as his zest for life allowed, standing in front of the cage watching the bird preening, juggling a sunflower seed with beak and tongue, clambering laboriously about the wire enclosure, pursuing other psittacine occupations. Sometimes Victor would utter the single syllable "warks" which more often than not the bird echoed, but whether Victor taught the parrot this enigmatic word or vice versa was uncertain. Actually it was quite capable of coherent English speech, its longest phrase being "Polly Fuller lives at Blackpool", the banality of this being accounted for if not excused by Leslie's family parrot, of the same breed, from the same source, having (save for the different surname) the same words on its black tongue.

151

I confuse Mrs. Sidey somewhat with a later landlady of my own, in the digs I had when I went south in the mid-thirties, so I could not be sure which lady had some artificial addition—in bulk or colouring or both—to her hair. It was from his mother that Victor had inherited those traits of his already mentioned (except that of limited discourse with parrots). But really all that has stuck firmly in the mind is her theological defence of a fly-blown piece of gammon, left over from breakfast, brought on for my lunch.

We were not awfully long at Mrs. Sidey's yet enough happened during that time to fill a lustrum of old age: like some weak monarch she gave her name to the epoch, remaining herself unmemorable. It was while we were there that I introduced my wife-to-be to my mother and brother, awkwardness lessened by the meeting taking place at a cinema—the Palace, as I recall, where Mons. Spiro could not have long ceased to be—to which the two brace of us had made separate ways. I think mutual awe attended the first encounter of future brother- and sister-in-law. By then (he would be fifteen or sixteen) my brother's character and appearance had altered from childhood rather more than might have been expected from the natural effects of time and biology. Messages on Christmas cards and the occasional letter from my mother's brother Fred sometimes include to this day an enquiry about the health and whereabouts of "Jack", never failing to give me a shock of recognition. Fred must be one of the few still alive who thus refer to my brother.

The character "Jack Fuller" was impish, verging on the irresponsible; the round face alert, blue eyes merry;

figure not to be called plump, but by no means exiguous. My mother used to say that playing out of doors he would lie on the pavement as though it were as clean and comfortable as her own sofas but this may have had the touch of exaggeration characteristic of her pronouncements about matters that particularly offended her, such as household dirt or personal shabbiness, just as in a similar context she may have played up the scruffiness of the young Willie Walton on the pavement outside his father's house. Jack always had a good many friends or acquaintances. At Miss Barraclough's I would be sent to look for him when he failed to turn up at his notional bedtime. There were half a dozen pavements he might be prostrate on, to say nothing of more *recherché* locations like Albert Griffiths's hut, this being at the rear of a butcher's shop kept by Griffiths *père*. In the hut, meat stolen by Albert or donated by his father was cooked in dripping that usually smelt as though not far from rancidity. Here perhaps were laid the foundations of my brother's notable future career in hotel and catering education, studies certainly needed by Albert Griffiths. At this epoch Jack went to the kindergarten I myself had attended, situated in a hall attached to a "Baptist Tabernacle", near the offices to which T. & F. Wylie Kay later moved.

Northlands High School—a girls' junior school as well as a kindergarten—was run with great efficiency by the proprietress, Miss Moorhouse, assisted by three able mistresses, Miss Arnott, Miss Proctor and Miss Schooler. Like the Boss, Miss Moorhouse had come from a region or class where Blackpool speech habits were alien. She

153

was tall, gracious, slightly stooping, her bun of grey hair with a faint threat of disintegration. When her pupils at the end of the school day had changed back into boots and shoes from the plimsolls compulsory in school, and were in their outdoor clothes ready to depart, Miss Moorhouse was always at the exit to say au revoir. "Goodbye, shrimps!" she used to cry to the youngest groups. My brother, already conscious of a proper, non-native style of speech and for once deviating from irresponsibility through the force of Miss Moorhouse's personality, would respond with a gentility hard to indicate phonetically: "Gudbye, Miss Meurherse!'

As to shrimps, after he had joined me at Seafolde House and I had become head house prefect, I beat him for eating that delicacy at a stall on the promenade. The incident encapsulates much of its epoch: the tradition of behaviour for boys wearing the school uniform; my dotty and priggish devotion to authority; my brother's early enterprise and gourmandism, the latter eventually international. It hardly needs saying that in later life I had to have the occasion recalled to me: the censor had expunged the memory.

After lingering a little with the Boss and Ettaboo and such as Meng, Thompson and Sage, my brother went on to King William's College in the Isle of Man, his educational milieu during the Sidey era. Spartan, games-orientated, it was not his cup of tea really but it opened up more vistas than could have been found at Seafolde House in its declining days. For instance, he had a housemaster and in the housemaster's study was the piano on which his relation Amy Woodforde-Finden had composed the "Indian Love Lyrics", familiar to us from parlour performances in Oldham, to say nothing of those in the Metropole lounge or on the North Pier. The drastic change of schools at an awkward age did nothing to settle him academically and he emerged at the end of his schooldays lacking both foundations and impulse for a conventional career. Like me, he needed the breathing-space and contacts with a wider world a university would surely have given. He had been a precocious reader of prose fiction, changing Christmas and birthday presents of children's books for the Russian classics, and the taste continued and widened. The boy encountered that night at the Palace Cinema was tall, handsome, with a flair for dressing well, far from the rancid-fat fryer of Albert Griffiths's hut. He was becoming, probably had already become, the Jekyll character "John Fuller".

I suppose a school in the Isle of Man being chosen for him to escape the decline and fall of Seafolde House was not totally divorced from our having previously holidayed on the island, initially prompted by a family connection. Sam Mills, the father of "Bone" (the girl my Uncle John married), was a stockbroker's clerk who lived in Oldham, in a house in Hollins Road, perhaps half a mile nearer Hollinwood than my grandparents' house. I went there as a boy with my uncle, probably to pick up my aunt-to-be for a Sunday afternoon walk preceding "tea" at my grandparents" (where the cheese and onions dish that was my grandfather's speciality might well be on the menu), a courtship ritual then common, perhaps still so. Though Sam Mills's house was a small old terrace house, the living-room reached directly by a step down from the street-door, it was said that he had done well in the cotton share boom. Whether he was caught in the dire slump that followed I do not know, but he had enough money to retire eventually to the Isle of Man. His house there was more commodious and we stayed in it at least once, perhaps as paying guests. He had become an obsessive vegetable grower. When boiled, his potatoes were like "balls of flour", the last word in his Oldham pronunciation strongly two-syllabled and the phrase permanently taking our fancy. The house was drained to a septic tank which he raided to manure his tomatoes. Or so tradition goes. Perhaps this was why on a subsequent holiday on the island we stayed elsewhere.

I missed two months of life with Mrs. Sidey and Victor through going to Gibson & Weldon's law classes in London immediately before my Intermediate. A like period was similarly spent before the Final (when, however, we had long left the semi-bungalow). To try to disentangle the two occasions, give some account of the good many extraordinary incidents and characters involved, seems at the moment beyond my will. I believe at the time I was wholly conscious that much of what was happening to me was fundamentally antipathetic, yet such is youth's vigorous acceptance of existence I adopted the life-style of others without much protest or attempted avoidance. But possibly even in this area a weakness, a wish not to offend, a fatal concern for third parties—cowardice of a kind—was operative and partly accounted for the strange life of sitting late in Soho cafés, fitfully but intensely getting to know enough law to qualify as a solicitor (the Intermediate in particular

156

having a high casualty rate), not to mention follies into which one was led by friends overbearing, slightly insane. I think, for instance, of removing collar and tie for pathetic effect (the separate collar surely dates the occasion as the earlier one), collecting for a friend singing in the gutter near the Angel rather more from daring than penury. Recently, in George Gissing's diaries (*London and the Life of Literature in Late Victorian England*), I came across this about his relationship with a travelling companion; an extreme case, no doubt, but one that struck home:

It would take an hour to write down all the things I do and say in one day, just to suit his variable moods and temper. Why do I regularly wash up all the things after meals? Why do I catch a bad cold waiting for him outside a shop where he is purchasing follies? Why do I stint myself of butter, that there may seem more for him? Not out of affection, most surely, but mere cowardice. I never dare say what I think, for fear of offending him, or causing a misunderstanding. And this has so often been the case in the course of my life. Therefore it is that I am never at peace save when alone.

As I write, I remember that still in the house are the letters I wrote to my future wife during both London absences, never perused since sent, which would probably allow a reasonably accurate narrative to be constructed, pinpointing my meetings with the then youthful writer Paul Potts, hearing the then Lady Mosley speak at a

New Party mass meeting, to say nothing of more self-revelatory occasions. That would be an exercise of literary art a deal different from what has so far been attempted—the inaccuracy of which I feel I must labour. I know from this and a little previous biographical writing, through checking references and through consultation with others, how staggeringly at fault my memory can be, a matter I will briefly return to later. Some matters here have been corrected, some not checked: what can be said in favour of things set down is that I believe them to be true—though occasionally it has struck me that I may well have misjudged mood, injecting into the past feelings I hold now. I mean, for instance, was I not possibly unhappier in early days about a life far from fulfilling its deepest and truest desires and gifts? Later, some sort of compromise was achieved and endured.

Apropos of the acceptance of quotidian existence, it hardly needs saying that a vital ingredient was literary ambition, albeit singularly ungratified. Time rolled by without periodical or any other kind of publication. I believe the first appearance of a poem of mine, the "dissolving pier" piece already sufficiently rescusitated, was in the *Sunday Referee*'s Poets' Corner, the name of the feature a sufficient indication of its dubiety, reinforced by the reward I received, namely a penknife. The thing has got into literary annals, however, through having published early work by Pamela Hansford Johnson, Julian Symons and Dylan Thomas. But the poem referred to could not have appeared before 1933. At various stages I hawked round collections of poems, in one of which Macmillans seemed genuinely if languidly interested. Still, the years from sixteen to twenty-two were pretty well a complete wash-out. Nor did the rest of the thirties bring any really measurable success. It never occurred to me I was in the wrong ball-game, though once, sending poems not for the first time to a decent but now forgotten paper called *Everyman*, I burst out in my covering letter: "Are these any good at all?" From the literary editor I had a sympathetic note—and the poems back.

I never stopped writing prose and verse, and trying to market it, but when recognition of a kind eventually arrived—far from that hoped for when my heroes were such as Wells and Chesterton—I was amazed by it nevertheless, as I would be now should a substantial readership or critical acclaim be suddenly bestowed. I was amazed at appearing in due course in *New Verse*, having admiringly witnessed its birth, just as after the War I was amazed at the evolution of my first novel into print. As was hoped for in the 220 System, when the hard nut of utter failure was expelled a series of modest successes followed, due really to the sympathy of editors, especially John Lehmann over many years, but also Julian Symons, J.R. Ackerley, Alan Ross, Anthony Thwaite, Karl Miller . . . I will not try to complete the list, for as I go on more names occur and to omit through forgetfulness would be unforgivable.

In a sense the wheel has already come full circle, since most of my books are now as though they had never been published—out of print, unlikely ever to be in print again, some novels indeed never achieving sales of more than two or three thousand copies, books of verse with

159

circulations even more exiguous. Such a destiny for my ambitions would have been beyond contemplation in pre-publication days—an irony of due Hardyesque proportions. Equally unforeseeable would have been the stoic or perhaps blasé attitude of old age to this odd state of affairs. Though the anxiety to write does not seem to fall off as one gets old, the notion hardens that one has proved a point simply by having in the end joined the ranks of the creators who engage the interest of some at least of those bound up in the strange pursuit of reading imaginative literature.

Bobby, the friend at whose suggestion I subscribed to the chamber concerts held in the Metropole lounge, was not of the race of truly devout readers, nor did his interest in me prove entirely intellectual. I suppose he was in his mid-thirties, which would make him, as I write this, less than likely to be still alive. There was a moment after the War when we could have met again, though we had been out of touch for—what?—fifteen years. The press must on some occasion have linked my literary and legal work and Bobby, being briefly in London, telephoned me at the office suggesting a meeting. Whatever the circumstances, no doubt militating against freeing myself at short notice, I ducked the invitation. I regret that. I would not have done it now, more adapted to dealing with such excessively non-routine occasions and, indeed, more capable of letting ordinary human feelings govern my actions, though that is not saying much.

When I wrote *The Perfect Fool* I assumed he was living, so the character in the novel who stands in for him is to a substantial degree invented. What I would say now is that though I had no interest in male friendships other than the "innocent" kind with Leslie, and at first obtusely imagined Bobby the same, his different affection was rarely and most tactfully indicated. I could not respond but that was the only embarrassment. And even had I possessed from the start more gumption, there was nothing to be done about the situation. Curious that in the three or four years that had elapsed since school, erotic activity with members of one's own sex had become unthinkable—not that at school it held any great attraction, simply that there a fairly uninhibited commerce existed at times at a certain age, not of the least emotional importance or complication.

I feel sure that Bobby sensed, as did I, some grave contradiction between his job and his persona. He was exceptionally well turned out and his manner *très comme il faut*. To the chamber concerts he used to bring an attractive widow, rather older than himself; and he holidayed abroad. But at other times, travelling for a firm of popular manufacturing chemists (a modern version of the character in the song, quoted later, often sung by my grandfather), he had to visit the little general shops of Lancashire, keeping them stocked up with acidosis remedies and the like, many such products being displayed on cards to which the phials of pills were attached on thin white-cotton-covered elastic. It may well have been that "Daisy" headache powders and "Lung Healers", specifics familiar from my infancy, were among those dealt with. He did not own a car so his itineraries were done by rail. Our first meeting was appropriately on the last train from Manchester, both bound from the

161

Hallé concert, brought into contact through a troublesome drunk in the same compartment, though I do not doubt Bobby had engineered his own presence. At the time of that episode we were still living at the flat but strangely enough on moving to Mrs. Sidey's I found myself quite near the house where he, too, lived in "rooms", to which I was occasionally invited. The house belonged to a member of his family and compared well in décor and comfort with Mrs. Sidey's, a good piano in Bobby's sitting-room notably impressing me, and I think photographs of antiquities on the walls.

Many years after the events narrated here the actress Jill Balcon brought home to me in conversation the utility of the curious, if not ludicrous, term "artiste" when discussing the theatrical profession (and even the appearance of poets in public, reading their own work; grisly entertainment) if employed with the right nuance. Fowler is correct in emphasising that despite the terminal "e" the expression is applicable to either sex: he adds that its use should be confined to "professional singer, dancer, or other public performer", with no implication "that the performance is in fact artistic". All the same, I think sophisticated usage nowadays confines the term to performers of a slightly old-fashioned cast, perhaps with mild versatility and a tendency to sentiment—troupers with a wide appeal, guaranteed to cause no offence.

Muriel George was an artiste. I do not remember, if I was ever told, how Bobby got to know her. By then middle-aged, she became even better known later in life when she played parts, usually vignettes, in more than a few British films. As I wrote those last words it occurred to me, as it had never done before, to look her up in Halliwell's indispensible *Filmgoer's Companion*, where I find the usual accurate and succinct professional characterization: "Plump, motherly British character actress who often played charladies or landladies. Music-hall background." According to Halliwell her film début was in 1932, the year after I was introduced to her by Bobby, which confirms my notion of her career. The *Companion* says she was born in 1883 so the "music-hall background" could well have been shared with such as Little Tich and Arnold Richardson. In fact Halliwell is referring to the inter-war years: before the First World War she was in the sort of show of which that on the Blackpool Central Pier (and in Happy Valley) was a hardy descendant. Her first appearance was as a young girl in Pélissier's famous pierrot troupe, when apparently she was already married to someone called Robin George. In the same epoch that marriage had come to an end and she married her second husband and stage partner, Ernest Butcher.

It must be stressed that the person I met was far from the Miss Barraclough or Mrs. Sidey type, despite the film parts she was about to play. In the past she must have been personable enough—not hard to imagine, though she could never have been a beauty—to contract two marriages and the possible union I shall refer to. Ernest Butcher was two or three years younger than her—a light comedian originally, I suppose—who in his songs and dialogue inclined to Mummerset. "British character actor who spent a lifetime playing mild little men", is the extent of Halliwell's characterisation; unusually, a trifle lacking in precision, for Butcher had

163

a long concert-party, if not music-hall, history, and I think his film career did not start until early in the Second World War.

My glimpse of this world was a result of Bobby taking me one evening to the summer show in the pavilion on the middle pier of Blackpool's three. Each had its individual entertainment, even class, character. The North Pier, befitting its position by the Metropole, had two pavilions: in the one on its head, Mons. Spiro (or his equivalent) conducted, as it might be, the Second Hungarian Rhapsody; at the end, before one descended to the jetty to fish for "dabs" or embark on a steamer that might ply round Morecambe Bay or even to the Isle of Man, there was a second pavilion where a fairly lavish summer show was mounted, the impresario being Lawrence Wright who under the famous *nom de plume* "Horatio Nicholls" (a name in the Blackpool parlance detested by the Boss coming out as "Oraysher Nittles") wrote many songs of the day, including "Souvenirs" and possibly "Shepherd of the Hills". At one time he lived conveniently at the Metropole, his riches presumably putting him on better terms than Miss Paine with the Prussian.

The pavilion on the southernmost pier, the Victoria Pier, was dominated in my time by an annual entertainment always starring Fred Walmsley, an elderly low comedian, funny, who in winter played pantomime dames and carried this side of his talent into the summer shows, a sketch particularly successful including a routine of undressing for bed, a voluminous nightdress being first put on and the day clothes taken off underneath it (a procedure not unrealistic, for I recall servants who used

164

to do just that). Always good for a laugh was his giving himself, with sighs of satisfaction, after bringing out a pair of corsets from under the nightdress, a thorough scratch round the ribs. To disgress further, when I was at boarding-school Blackpool staged a carnival modelled on the one at Nice. The notion was to vivify the late spring so as to entice visitors before the crowded high season, but the municipality had not weighed the difference in climate at that time of year between Mediterranean and Irish Sea. The carnivals had their successes, possibly mainly of an unofficial saturnalian kind, but a *bataille des fleurs* on the exposed promenade I suppose did not attract great masses or give great pleasure. Even in the start of the official theme song of the second (and last) carnival might be detected, pondering the epithet and the indication of untimely repetition, a disillusioned or wearied undertone:

> Hello, hello, hello, breezy Blackpool,
> It's Blackpool carnival time again.

When war broke out at last in 1939 (and though I had then been agonizedly anti-fascist for a long time) I was quite shocked at the sudden appearance of vulgar broadsheets against Hitler. In a similar way the Blackpool carnivals released forces that the good taste and manners of the time had hitherto forbade public expression; one manifestation being the sale on the streets, among the carnival crowds, of a small paper called *Billy's Weekly Liar*. The title indicates a periodical nature but it had never come my way before and its surprising contents influenced my own publication, *The Feats of Dormitory Three*, previously referred to; though I did not dare to be as scatological. The literary genre exploited by *Billy's Weekly Liar* that I particularly admired was the cod library list, containing such books as *The Tiger's Revenge* by Claude R. Sole, *My Life in a Nudist Colony* by I. Seymour Cox and *The Passionate Lover* by E. Tudor Tittiov (the last-named a somewhat implausible Anglo-Russian *mélange*).

The grandparents of Byng, Gorill's tormentor, had a largish house on the promenade, not far from the school, and the boarders were invited to view the carnival procession from the front garden. The Carnival King (or, more likely, Queen) was none other than Fred Walmsley, and when the float bearing him and his consort passed, the comedian stood up, sceptre raised, and called: "Three cheers for Seafolde House!" The assembled boarders (though, if anything like me, stunned at this royal attention) responded heartily. How had Fred Walmsley been put on to doing it? The idea of the Boss sitting through the nightdress routine to go backstage afterwards to make a request for a commercial, so to speak, was not on the cards, despite his later attendance at the Palace Varieties. In fact, I guess that behind the business was Byng's family, who had music-hall connections, his uncle being Percy Honri, always billed as "A concert-in-a turn", the subtitle cleverly alluding to both his principal instrument and musical prowess in general.

The entertainment on the Central Pier, though in the part of Blackpool appealing most to the proletarian holiday-makers of the summer Wakes weeks, was usually
166

mid-way in tone between the other two pier shows. What Muriel George and Ernest Butcher were starring in was essentially a pierrot show or concert party, such as my Uncle John had figured in as the soubrette during the First World War. The convention still held that though the cast was in pierrot costume in the first half, in the second evening dress was *de rigueur*. The two stars did well in the sketches, as borne out by their later careers in the cinema, and their own "spot", late in the second half, rather surprisingly largely featuring folk songs, was put over well. Afterwards, Bobby took me to their dressing-room, the journey itself giving an exciting sense of eminently exploitable literary material of a kind never before met. How typical, absurd and forgivable of him to introduce me to Muriel George as a slavish admirer to whom he would find it incongruous—impossible—because of the youthful charms that had helped to captivate me, to explain a stout figure lurking in the shadows of the dressing-room. It says a good deal for Bobby's social graces that all this was insinuated rather than laid on the line, which, however, did not make it much less embarrassing for me who at that time would be quite unpracticed in dealing with drama (or flannel) imported without warning into small talk (even today relishing it not at all).

The figure on the dressing-room's periphery was Muriel George's son, John Davenport. Who his father was I do not know. There was an Arthur Davenport who wrote the lyrics for Pélissier's songs but I fancy there is no more than coincidence in that. I heard it said that John's one-time affluence came from his father, who

167

may well in fact have been Muriel George's first husband, John avoiding his mother's stage name. At this date he was or lately had been a Cambridge undergraduate. The uncertainty arises from his having appeared in and helped to edit *Cambridge Poetry 1929* which marks him as already having been up for three years. Of course, he may have been in for a fourth year, which would be consonant with his incongruously frittering away part of the Long Vacation in Blackpool. In later years he put on more weight but even when I first knew him he was notably solid, a stout man of the formidable rather than genial kind. His brown hair was cut and brushed in schoolboy style (and I mean without the oleaginous or adhesive auxiliaries used by such as Matley) above a flat face. Bulldog Drummond is introduced as ugly but attractive, a rather literary concept which John, however, could be said to embody. On me he made an impression hardly to be over-emphasised. I put him in an unfinished novel of the epoch and in a romanticised guise he even appears in a fiction I wrote some time after the war called *Fantasy and Fugue*. At that first encounter some literary talk was exchanged and a further meeting arranged. The initiative would have come from him, for, as already laboured, I was as green as grass. Almost certainly Bobby must have given warning that I was a budding writer, so John could not have looked forward to my introduction with any relish. But I can see that he was patient and kindly behind an exterior already tough, to grow more so over the years. On my side, exchanges with one of greater literary sophistication—indeed, vis-à-vis the new poetry perhaps less than a score of people

168

of equal knowledge could at that time have been found—was remarkably decisive. I do not suppose we met more than half a dozen times that summer, nor do I recall much of what was said (probably did not hear a good deal of it, for he had a habit of speaking quietly or into open space or extremely allusively), yet my endeavours in art were permanently altered.

Four books I bought initially through his commending them: the *Cambridge Poetry* already mentioned; the *Oxford Poetry* of 1930, because it contained poems by Stephen Spender; Edgell Rickword's *Invocation to Angels*; and Auden's 1930 *Poems*. It says much for the standard of service of the day that all these, mostly cheap, mostly from small publishers, were ordered from and promptly supplied by Sweeten's, Blackpool's virtually sole bookshop. (F.P. Sweeten, tall, grey, stooping, giving personal attention to any customer not yet shelling out, was a character like the Boss, capable of inducing fear, though willing to do a financially advantageous deal with my brother over the *Greyfriars Holiday Annual* and Dostoevsky). The drama of coming across for the first time the work of Rickword, Empson, Spender, Auden, *et al*, though stirring must not be exaggerated. The penny took a little time really to drop. John Davenport himself was remarkably open-minded about recent generations. For example, when I foolishly wrote off Flecker (whom I would then have thought it correct to regard as outworn compared with the Sitwells, say) he said he thought Flecker quite a good poet. I expect this would be a relief of a kind, for I had admired Flecker and having been thus reassured, went on reading him. I think I had a

169

growing sense that I must write poetry whose aim was not "beauty" of the kind for which Flecker supplied notable touchstones, but the touchstones went on being touched:

> Then the grey square of wall should fade away,
>
> And glow again, and open, and disclose
>    The shimmering lake in which the planets swim,
> And all that lake a dewdrop on a rose.

When I opened Rickword's marvellous book I found at once beauty pretty well of the kind accustomed to:

> Trees have been named and brutes with shining skins,
> and in pure darkness many a planet spins
> no living eyes have seen, yet men say *There
> Orion's gathering-in his massy hair* . . .

The same thing could be said about some of Spender's five poems in *Oxford Poetry 1930*:

> The trumpets were curled away, the drum beat no
>    more.
> Only the Swan the Swan danced in my brain:
> All night she spun; drooped, lifted again;
> Bent and arched her arms; sunk on the frore
> Snow-brittle feathers skirting her . . .

But I suppose (though in the absence of documentation the *post hoc* rationalisation may be wildly askew) that elsewhere Rickword's disillusion and Spender's poem about unemployment helped the concept of a poetry of direct social function, having to do with life in a wider and more down to earth way than the provision of stimulating or consolatory sounds and images. This was confirmed in a nevertheless somewhat baffling way by the Auden book. What on earth did one's uninstructed mind make of it in 1931? No doubt, as in so much of Auden, there was immediate recognition of a life one had lived oneself:

> On Sunday walks
> Past the shut gates of works

—recalling Mr. Tregenza holding his hat on in the breeze, and a remoter past in Oldham. Many of my current preoccupations were expressed in startlingly-employed traditional forms:

> Lawrence, Blake and Homer Lane, once healers in
> our English land;
> These are dead as iron for ever; these can never hold
> our hand.

Still, I am sure I used the book to some extent as I had used books of poems in the past—to discover in them mottos for my own life, and those special bits of poetic poetry—though things like Lawrence's *Nettles* may already have convinced me that writing poetry was not a matter of trying to create beauty. Above all, the Auden book may have stressed the need for a new life, to come

171

out of difficult, probably violent, struggle. I should add that Auden sanctioned in me, as in many, obscurity, so that even though he perhaps helped towards a verse of social and political directness, I had largely worked through that by the time my first collection of poems, published early in 1939, was made up. A good deal of that volume was "clotted" or "thick", the critical adjectives we often used for what nonetheless often seemed an inescapable style in the confused and doomed later years of the decade.

In my account of my initial relationship with John Davenport there will be as many gaps and as much dubious history as in what I have said of his introduction to me of my own generation of poets. I see us sitting at a table in a largish bar on the pier—a room of windows and cast-iron decorated pillars—at some hour when it was little patronised. I drank scarcely at all in those days: going into a bar would never have occurred to me. A dull companion I must have been for John, who liked a drink then, though I expect not so much as in later life. I remember, too, going one morning to the pier pavilion and finding him at one of the two pianos that on a lower level flanked the stage, the pianist of the show at the other, playing the solo (or perhaps the arrangement of the orchestral part) of a Bach keyboard concerto. I like to think that the troupe's excellent tenor was also knocking about, making some highbrow contribution to the proceedings, but cannot be sure: he was a young man called Webster Booth. I must have seen the show, or parts of it, several times, for I can recall some of the songs—concerted numbers from the whole cast and items from the repertoire of Muriel George and Ernest Butcher. I see from Halliwell that they both died in 1965, a mere coincidence, for their marriage had been dissolved during the War and Ernest Butcher had a new wife, the sister of a famous ventriloquist of the epoch. John himself only outlived his mother by a year.

After the War I encountered him on a number of occasions. On the first I feel sure I referred to our meeting in bygone days in one of those Blackpool edifices "whose minarets were charcoaled on the sky". By this date he was bigger, more formidable, almost certain to have a few drinks on board. I did not press him when he failed, I think pretty well completely, to respond to this jogging of his memory. In the event we never discussed former times. I did not realise then that some are cagy about their past: it may fail ignominiously to correspond with a past they have created in their own or the public mind. In John's case, being up at Cambridge with Lehmann and Empson and Eberhart and James Reeves and Michael Redgrave and Hugh Sykes Davies and Basil Wright and Bronowski and Julian Bell, and putting their poems together in an anthology, may in retrospect have seemed real, while his mother taking part in the action song "One finger and thumb keep moving" not at all an actual part of his past. Thinking of the time he spent as a liver of the poetic life among Blackpool's insanities, who can blame him? Of course, it could well have been he had completely forgotten meeting the aspiring, near teetotal provincial poetaster.

Though by the time of these encounters of the second kind I had made a reputation which despite its modesty

173

he would certainly have been aware of (for even as an undergraduate his knowledge of literary affairs was encyclopoedic) he did not refer to that either. Slightly surprising, then, when at a party he came quite amiably up to me. I was already talking to Stephen Spender and said something fatuous-sounding, such as: "You two know each other, of course." To John, Stephen said (I give an approximation of his words): "Yes, I know you and what you have been saying about my brother, my entire family." He was extremely cross. John immediately moved away, though quite capable, with far less prompting, of initiating a physical kerfuffle, as happened at Bernard Gutteridge's rather smart wedding reception. I think by way of palliation I told Stephen (or perhaps I merely wished I had) that even before he had published his first Faber collection John had been a propagandist for his poetry.

When *The Death of the King's Canary*, a cod detective story John had written with Dylan Thomas in 1940, was belatedly published in 1976, the writer of the introduction said that in the very early thirties John was a poet compared by his contemporaries to Auden, Spender and Day Lewis, but this was not so. Some claimed to have prognosticated difficulties on seeing his long poem in *Cambridge Poetry 1929*, ominously subtitled "A Fragment". I must have recognised that it blatantly employed the styles of Rickword, Eliot and Sacheverell Sitwell, to name but three: nevertheless, I liked its knowing turns and references—and, truth to say, the lingering nineties sense of verbal "beauty":

Now that the year is shifting in its bed
Adonis-like in petal-feathered sheen
the boar, dark winter's domination ended,
the earliest shoots of April can be seen;
save in interminable pale ending streets
where dazedly the poet now repeats—
an atom before a tracery of steel
cylinders, dynamoes, pistons, wheel on wheel—
the names Picasso, Cocteau, Schoenberg . . .

To put the case crudely, over-sophistication was in those days John's trouble, the opposite of my own. He did not recover: at his death he was really known only for his *Observer* book reviews, though whether one will be remembered oneself for anything more weighty must be doubted. However, on our re-encounter he may have been embarrassed to be apparently overhauled in a contest in which he had seemed to start with such an advantage. On the other hand, and perhaps more likely, the thought may never have crossed his clever and obstreperous mind.

Characteristic of what was crammed into the relatively short sojourn at Mrs. Sidey's was starting to smoke, a habit more gripping than booze and which lasted until my early sixties, invariable accompaniment of work, pleasure, hurt. I picked up one of my mother's "Craven A" cigarettes, then actually cork-tipped, without filter, and lighting it, as I had seen done, with an ember held in the fire-tongs, remarked: "I think I'll start smoking." The action and phrase had been meditated. Characteristic that my mother's mild opposition should have been on

175

the ground of expense but who at that time linked smoking directly with death?

After Mrs. Sidey's, despite the continuance of memory's blanks and blunders, autobiographical material becomes more abundant, involving greater difficulties of selection, chronology, frankness. Would it be too simplistic to try to deal with it in the manner that has served so far? In any event I am sure my memory is morbidly defective. I used to say being a solicitor had trained me to forget facts and remember sources, practical and effective knowledge of the law being a nose for retrieval rather than a grasp of detail, the ability (to use a better metaphor) to hear faint bells ringing. Though that may have been my working method as a lawyer it does not explain the deficiency. Someone (I forget who!) once remarked that memory was self-justification. Again, that would not explain my case, for though the subconscious no doubt operates to allow a certain quota of guilt, gaffes, failures and wrong turnings to hide in oblivion, a good few are still vivid, often pondered, as will have been seen.

Perhaps a sharper memory (and additional stamina; the lack of that in a physical sense indicated by my jibbing at the mile) would have led me to write fiction incorporating more of the material reality of life, demanding to be densely and quite extensively delineated mainly in terms of character and social class. These are Dickensian categories, and whenever I read Dickens I am struck afresh by the apparent sureness of his knowledge of social traits—clothes, food, servants, the role in the family of its subsidiary members, money, reading matter, details of places of public resort. Mere caricature pertains, of course, when the aristocracy is offered to be depicted; and the sureness may falter in the ranks of the upper middle-class, but elsewhere all is copper-bottomed. Even in *Boz* and the early parts of *Pickwick* the knowledge is richly at work. It is the knowledge gained by the mobile petty-bourgeois, which I was from my earliest days. It implies a sensitivity to habits, behaviour and appearances in English society, things that have always played a large part in our literary art. George Orwell lacked it and some of those he has influenced, such as the new novelists of the fifties, recklessly disregarded it. TV drama, so susceptible of being an inferior art, goes on getting things wrong; regional accents and their consistency within a single piece, for example. And when my novel *Image of a Society* was dramatised for TV I was pained to see the second or third executive in a large provincial building society washing the dishes, and in an apron. In literature truth about life cannot be attempted without truth about society, which is where much post-war fiction and drama is shaky, though the deficiency may be common in feebler writers in all epochs.

# 8.  Kind Doddy

Inevitably, in the course of writing, detached memories have arisen not easy to fit in their proper place; some in fact seeming to have a special right to appear as after-thoughts or in isolation. "Musical fruit" my grandfather called peas, even garden peas, the joke (when I had divined or, more likely, had explained to me its vulgar point) capable of effective repetition, like a line of poetry whose observation or trope, originally startling, remains operant when utterly familiar. As has been seen, my grandfather was not loathe to repeat sayings, quotations, actions, a trait I inherited, possibly have inadvertently exhibited here. I used in *The Perfect Fool* his complaint or boast about having to go to see Gandhi at a time when the Indian nationalist leader was especially troublesome, the person involved eventually proving, however, to live on the Fylde coast, by name Gandy and an executor with my grandfather for a mutual relative. My grandfather was alert to puns and alliteration and so forth—a sort of poetic sensitivity, so I must not think that side of my nature comes exclusively from my grandmother. He always liked to say the name of a friend of his, Corny (short for Cornelius) Kershaw; perhaps his bridge partner on that night of my unannounced visit. "She has a voice like a cinder under a door," I once heard him observe, I seem to think apropos Keck's singing prowess, though this notable simile may not have been original. Both here and in the novel referred to I have given the recipe for pineapple icecream, which, like Constant Lambert in *Façade*, he used to deliver in a tempo of virtuoso rapidity, copied from the market-place. Another phrase of similar origin was "Pies or cakes or pop!"—also prestissimo. Interest in market hucksters perhaps helped to determine the siting of his office near Tommyfield. A song he sang about such a character must have come from the music-hall of an era long before he was Superintendent Registrar of Births, Marriages and Deaths, however:

> Oh my eye, oh my eye!
> Anyone ill, anyone ill?
> Oh my eye!
>
> For he's a jolly good chap, chap, chap,
> And he carries a pack on his back.
> He's plasters and pills to cure all ills
> And they call him "Medicine Jack".

A line from another of his songs became fixed in my

memory because of what I regarded as the brilliance of its literary allusion: "They call her 'Monkey Brand' because she won't wash clothes." I was familiar with the line before the proprietory article in question—which was a hardish oblong cake of cleansing material. Imagine my pleased astonishment, akin to opening *Hamlet* for the first time, when I found, on the paper wrapper that "Monkey Brand" came in, the legend "Won't wash clothes"—an implied boast of the article's utility in all other such affairs of life, which the lyric-writer had adroitly turned to characterize a lazy housewife, whom my upbringing would anyway be more than ready to scorn.

For years I used a saying of my grandfather's when refusing a second (or third) helping: "No, thank you. I've had an elegant sufficiency." The epithet always bothered me by its seeming inappropriateness—until much later in life I found the words in Thomson's *The Seasons*. But I have never discovered the source of the phrase "lucky bargees" ("Come on, you lucky bargees," he used to call when offering chocolates to his grand-children), though "bargee" appears in *Stalky & Co.* in an affectionate as well as a pejorative context. Also remaining mysterious is a sentence he employed to indicate any substance, usually food, either of a strangish nature or the name of which he could not immediately bring to mind. "I'll have some of that scanamanah, commonly known as lobjaw," he would say, confronted by a choice of pudding. Possibly the words, here neces-sarily indicated phonetically, were of his own invention. Almost equally esoteric was his crying "Ee, diddle,
180

diddle' in a loud soprano voice in my grandmother's ear when he came down (unshaved, collarless, wearing a neckerchief) and kissed her, feigning to menace with his bristling chin, before sitting at the breakfast table. I used to wonder whether her annoyance was real or assumed, part of the act. The syllable "Ee", very much a feature of the speech of east Lancashire (pertaining, indeed, to Yorkshire) has also an enigmatic quality. At one time my brother and I had picked up and frequently used a phrase which my mother in the end characterised as near swearing and forbade. This was "Ee 'eck an' aye"; as broad in its expressive purposes as Miss Barraclough's "Dearie me today".

A joke not my grandfather's own which nevertheless pleased him concerned the subterranean public lavatories by the Oldham Theatre Royal, an amenity he worked long to bring into being and which immediately became known as Alderman Broadbent's two-valve receiver, the wireless allusion being prompted in regard to the technical specification by the feature of twin glazed domes above ground to admit the light. His occupation would confirm him in a temperament likely, as I think was the case, to take a Sweeneyesque view of human life.

My memory of the house at Waterhead, scene of so much distress (shared by my grandparents, who were there when my father's death was announced to me, probably when it occured), is not so nebulous as may have been implied. The steep garden, though by no means large, was wooded on its lower levels, always somewhat mysterious, and leading to a side entrance. That would be the way my brother and I went out on

181

to "the moors", where I would frighten him with a tale of a nearby boggart, and then run away. The yard at the back of the house my father had had asphalted and there I played with my scooter. I had coveted such a vehicle (probably Marjorie Marsland owned one) and my father had mine made by the carpenter at the rubber-proofing mill. The result was heavy, unhandy, with solid wooden wheels, perhaps even iron-shod. I see myself inexpertly battling with it in the yard but not for worlds would I have admitted its deficiencies, being then as now anxious through some species of embarrassment (for myself and for any vis-à-vis) to underplay disaster, even to find good in it. When my mother, in tears, embraced me on that Sunday morning of my father's death, I discovered something irrelevant to say or do—a message, or a sweet passed on to my brother, from my great-uncle Newton with whom I had been to church, being told about my father on returning, though aware before that because of a boy I knew saying on my way home that our blinds were down and asking if there had been a death—my reply characteristically a denial, advancing spring-cleaning as the cause, however unlikely a week before Christmas.

Newton Broadbent was an elder brother of my grandfather's, a County Councillor—I do not know what his occupation was or had been—I think already a widower, his children grown up. He lived at Lees, a mile or so away, thus coming somewhat into our Waterhead existence. Possibly it was merely to get me out of the way during my father's illness—on the Sunday in question, during his last hours—that I walked to Great-uncle

Newton's house to accompany him to the church he would presumably have attended without my presence. I pause, suddenly thinking this might have been my mother's regard for my sensitivity over the painful months, remembering my stepfather telling me after my mother's death nearly thirty years later, of her pity for my "sad, beautiful face" (I come out with the phrase as showing her unself-regarding love, making more or less irrelevant the conventionalities her character had hardened into in later years)—the visage in question being shown at her bedside when her own carcinoma had been diagnosed. I wonder, too, if I would be able to bring to mind the procedure with Great-uncle Newton had not that Sunday morning been engraved on it by my father's dying and death.

Some routine at any rate had been established over my visits to Newton Broadbent's house. I would be shown into a small parlour, spick and span, full of knick-knacks, the style far from that of my father's furbishing of the Waterhead house. My great-uncle would soon appear, tall (as he seemed, perhaps was, unlike my grandfather), stout, in a frock-coat, the sweets in question (probably "ju-jubes") kept in a small box in a waistcoat pocket. I think we had one apiece as we walked hand in hand to church, he in a truncated top-hat. Certainly the box appeared and was offered before the sermon, a civilised gesture, perhaps of family antiquity. I fancy Newton was a sidesman or other officer: hence, maybe, the formal clothes. Newton was his (and my grandfather's) mother's maiden name: my Uncle John (whose second Christian name was also Newton) possessed a genealogical table which began with "Henry Newton of Lees, slater", who died in 1661, so for nearly 300 years the family had hung around those parts, crawling up in the world.

One fairly soon became conscious of being oneself a witness to change, if not yet acutely felt as bodily decay. While at Waterhead, the dressmaker measuring my mother pronounced that to fulfil fashion the skirt should be ten inches off the ground, a height that seemed as daring as the thirty miles an hour in the Ford with the English body later on. I remember being taken to the unveiling of a memorial, on a site towards Mumps, to the dead of the First War. When I first went to boarding-school, the handyman, with a species of palsy we used to imitate, was said to have been reduced to such wreckage through shell-shock. While we were at Mrs. Sidey's a fresh cast was once more assembling: it would help me to act out the few years of ineffectual work for peace, employment and the downfall of fascism before I left for Kent, and, soon after, I was living in London, as long desired. But on the heels of that was the start of the Second World War: my wife and son came to Blackpool for refuge, and before hostilities had ended my son was attending Northlands High School, now conducted by Miss Arnott and Miss Proctor, Miss Moorhouse having some time before said a last farewell to her shrimps.

The fresh cast referred to might be described as a blend of Isherwood and Upward, the latter predominant—such as the communist snack-bar owner; the declassed intellectual who served in it, member of that strange, in many ways admirable, sect, the SPGB; the skilled worker, CPGB member, forced to take work digging trenches for the Corporation gas department; the young Trotskyist grammar-school master—variously to die of self-neglect; to go bonkers on and off; to go south and make armaments; to be killed in the Spanish Civil War; to decline into marriage and a species of respectability. Even I myself, sheltered from many evils, virtually joined the ranks of the unemployed before I left for the south-east; an apt irony, for in the latter days of my articles I watched with guilt from an office window some friends in a feeble procession I had helped the National Unemployed Workers Movement to organize but which it was tolerantly recognized I was in the wrong social position to join myself.

Ideological turns followed each other as did historical turns. Psychoanalysis struck Seafolde House in 1927, when I heard two young masters discussing it, but though it plainly constituted a powerful and still more or less private key to the riddle of human existence I was not then tempted to look into it. I can still vaguely recall titles and authors mentioned (Freud and Jung not among them, the masters having already moved into esotericism), the word "id" familiar, though for years I should have been as stumped at defining it as spelling cupboard when I first met the Boss. One of the masters concerned was in fact his nephew. He it was whose genius had cast Gorill as Hippolyta, who had lent me Ian Hay and O. Henry and was to measure my record long jump, perhaps generously, for it was a leap so notable for those times as to earn a paragraph in the local paper. Having the same surname as the Boss he was always referred to by his first Christian name. Mr. David was handsome and

185

a good teacher, like his uncle, and with a facetiousness and sarcasm that despite being schoolmasterish was always good-humoured, going down well with me. "Stop exercising your prosimian propensities," he would say—to Byng as likely as not. Until recently the adjective had always been a slight puzzle: would not "simian" have sufficed? Then I looked up the word and found it described the order of lemurs, not apes. Presumably Mr. David knew this and was identifying a particular type of restless and mischievous animality—unless he had uncomprehendingly taken over a rotund phrase invented by someone else, like "terminological inexactitude". As to simian, I heard mentioned the other day a district of Manchester called Whalley Range, which was where Byng's home was and which in my schooltime fantasies I took to be an area of bare hills like the Mappin Terrace at the Zoo, and perhaps similarly of artificial construction, where during the holidays Byng capered about with the rest of his monkey-faced family.

If my early life has seemed to consist mainly of surfaces at least the reader has not had to suffer more nebulous speculations. When eventually I read him, Freud's account of the hidden life seemed to me strikingly plausible and illuminating. No doubt his models of the mind will seem medieval to subsequent generations but his connective insights and literary genius inspired me long into the post-Second War era. When we were very young, probably still at Waterhead, I used in bed to tell my brother John stories about a character called "Baby Bronco", a human baby not a foal of the Wild West. Where did the name come from? There is (or was) a
186

lavatory paper with the brand name "Bronco": is it too fanciful to see in my choice of nomenclature an infantile confusion between babies and faeces, as in Freud's Little Hans case history? And was I perhaps, to assuage some felt guilt, resurrecting my brother George, whose birth and death had occurred between my own birth and John's?

In the *TLS* not long ago, Maurice Richardson (soon afterwards to die, alas) quoted a dictum by an early convert to psychoanalysis, Dr. Eder: "We are born mad. We acquire morality and become stupid and unhappy. Then we die." It is an arguable view of life, not shared by me who believes, as these pages must have made plain, in the rule of the super-ego, mixed blessing though it may be. That is not to derogate from the power of the id which, indeed, some would see as the source of the renewals and developments of creativity which have sustained—helped to make not unhappy—my life. Soon after I first went to boarding-school I had a nightmare which sent me, crying out, running over the adjoining dormitory beds before I was fully awake and scurried back to my own where, when the light went on and some wakened boys discussed the bizarre event, I pretended to be asleep. In the morning I dared not face quizzing and mockery, and went on feigning sleep or a dozy illness as the others dressed, being eventually visited by the Headmaster's sister (who in those days was matron) as someone reported sick, perhaps dotty . . .

It has now come to me why "Uncle Alf" was so generous with gramophone records—and why, when I qualified as a solicitor, he bought me a gown, bands in

187

a green leather case, and a barrister's blue bag to transport them in. An uneasy conscience about shares acquired too cheaply I doubt was in point. He was my godfather, a relationship then as meaningful as in the Mafia now, even for the irreligious; and which I see as of some account, like a good few vanished things bordering on the sentimental. In this and similar matters my grandfather's formula is relevant. If, he said often in the days of my childhood, watching the domestic disposal of his purchased prize specimen, when you cut yourself a piece of cheese you included a due proportion of the rind you were a conservative; if your helping was rindless you were a radical. He did not obtrude his own convictions of right and wrong in the matter, content with pronouncing after the event on the politics or cast of mind thus in Freudian manner revealed. According to the cheese test I seemed at first to be a dyed in the wool radical. Yet soon some overmastering puritanical or parsimonious inclination turned me, in the realm of cheese, into a conservative, conscious of virtue in leaving for those to follow me neat right-angles and a proper share of sustenance. Darwin tells of his son, nicknamed Doddy, who "when two years and three months old . . . gave his last bit of gingerbread to his little sister, and then cried out, with high self-approbation 'Oh kind Doddy, kind Doddy.' " Thus perhaps was I at a similar age; only later my concern for others and desire to be thought good assuming, through shyness and so forth, chilly and convoluted forms.

The "detached memories" spoken of must be regarded as ever carried forward, part of the running total, but not always getting itemised. Thinking of Marjorie Marland's dislike of long black stockings, for instance, reminded me of an almost pathological hatred I had at the same epoch for my "sou'wester"—a black mackintosh headgear, like that worn by the sailor holding the giant codfish on the label of the also detested "Scott's Emulsion". Were the weather too inclement to prevent me from getting out of wearing it, I was agonizingly embarrassed at being seen in it and, if alone, took it off, rolled it up, and put it in my pocket until I was back in sight of home. The misery conferred was equalled in later life, at Seafolde House, by a pair of shoes, always too small for me. In the shop I had deluded myself about this defect, for the shoes had been reduced in price and I wanted my mother to have the advantage of the bargain. The reason for the reduction was plain (though I also glossed over this at the time): the toe-caps were curiously (and unfashionably) blunt and bulbous—unbecoming as well as too short for my feet. Unlike the sou'wester, one needed no phobia to want to discard them. Being new, they came up from the school cellars on Sundays only, but even this hebdomadal wearing was torture enough since the day's programme included a march to church and the Sunday afternoon walk. Such sparse pleasures as that routine afforded crippledom diluted (and one event good for a suppressed laugh was, I may mention, spotting the arrival at church of a regular worshipper crudely but accurately christened "Big Conk", the very person later played bridge with at Wilton Parade, Mrs. Laycock). Not for many weeks, perhaps a few terms even, did I have the enterprise to go illegally into the

189

cellars on Sundays and get (and subsequently return) my weekday shoes from the rows laid out for cleaning by the shell-shocked handyman. I would have promptly sacrificed the sou'wester but the comedian's shoes I persevered with—surely a constriction of my character induced by the intervening events of life.

Far more tenuous than such remembered facts is one's sense of the disappearing perspectives of people known, experiences undergone—richness that doesn't know why it has faded. Sometimes we used to visit my (or, rather, my mother's) Aunt Polly, a good tram-ride or car-ride from Hollins Road. Aunt Polly was my grandmother's (I think elder) sister; lived in pretty humble circumstances. Dimly I recall humorous interplay between them; and Aunt Polly's strong-charactered daughter, in whose life there was, or was to come, some such tragedy as an illegitimate child. But here memory is merging into something like dream. Was he from my grandmother's or grandfather's family the marbleless man who sat on the sofa in the front room at Hollins Road and occasionally ejaculated the word, or words, "Cat's-piss"? And was I there?

Analagous to the rediscovery of the Mumps drapers, Buckley & Proctor, was recently reading in the first volume of Dodie Smith's autobiography of the multiple grocers—multiple in the Manchester area—Seymour Meads, a name for me of perhaps greater antiquity and reconditeness, whose euphonious syllables possibly my grandfather took every opportunity of repeating as in the of Corny Kershaw, and but for that chance reading surely lost to my mind for ever. But what is to remind me of blanks truly vital?